Updating the Indelible:
Fear Memory Resolution and Healing through Psychotherapy

Updating the Indelible:
Fear Memory Resolution and Healing through Psychotherapy

Marie A. Wilson,
M.D.

UPDATING THE INDELIBLE:
FEAR MEMORY RESOLUTION AND HEALING THROUGH PSYCHOTHERAPY

Copyright © 2021, Marie A. Wilson, M.D.

Published by Marie A. Wilson, M.D., Edmonton, Canada

Paperback ISBN - 978-1-77354-291-1
eBook ISBN - 978-1-77354-292-8

This book is dedicated to my children
who have taught me how to be the best parent I could be,
and to my clients,
who missed out on the best parenting
and allowed me to learn how to help them help themselves.

Foreword

Having taken Dr. Marie Wilson's workshop on The Re-Definition of Self Process offered at the Society for Clinical and Experimental Hypnosis workshops and scientific sessions, I feel privileged to write a Foreword to her new book Updating the Indelible: Fear Memory Resolution and Healing through Psychotherapy. Dr. Wilson has tackled a major question facing therapists who provide therapeutic services for individuals presenting with traumatic issues. Are the traumatic memories indelibly imprinted in an individual's neural circuitry or is it possible to facilitate a lasting therapeutic change to the brain pathways within which the trauma has been imprisoned? As a physician specializing in Psychotherapy, Dr. Wilson used her medical acumen to seek an answer to this question.

Dr. Wilson makes a very strong case that the neural pathways can be changed so as to allow the individual receiving treatment to live a life free of traumatic memories rooted in early childhood memories or in recent or past extraordinary and damaging events.

With her professional roots in Medicine, Psychotherapy, and Ericksonian Hypnosis, Dr. Wilson writes of focusing on the therapeutic journey rather than having an endpoint that therapy strives to attain with the client. Through a comprehensive under-standing of the client, together with an awareness of taking them back to early primitive landmarks, often in their childhood, she guides the reader through this process.

In outlining the indelible nature of traumatic memories, she begins by discussing the manner in which maladaptive behaviors and beliefs are formed as a result of early childhood experiences. With the importance of biological survival being ever present in a growing infant, Dr. Wilson speaks to the importance of not judging the development of various maladaptive behaviors. Rather, she advocates using therapy to move the client to a place of cognitive understanding and emotional letting go as a way of facilitating a rewiring within which the traumatic memories were originally encrypted. Her book offers further discussion of the basic elements of memory formation, the lability of memories and a brief analysis of research that has been shown to interfere with the consolidation of traumatic memories. This description provides the necessary stepping-stones to assist the reader in understanding the rationale behind Dr. Wilson's thesis that traumatic memories are not indelible and are amenable to positive and lasting change.

In Chapter Three, Dr. Wilson lays out the systematic approach that she has developed and refined from her own clinical experience and training. Her personal belief in the inner drive inherent in our clientele to live more productive, happier, and rewarding lives – their own search for authenticity as it were – is very apparent. Discussions about how Systems Theory is played out, both intra- and interpersonally in clients, adds theoretical underpinnings to her therapeutic approach. The important use and awareness of Ericksonian hypnosis in her therapeutic approach underscores the importance of sensitivity and respect she has when dealing with the inner workings of a client's unconscious mind. She outlines the specific steps and exercises for the therapist to follow when assisting the client in changing the memory traces and beliefs that have maintained the client's trauma.

In the closing chapters, she focuses on the relationship of attachment to one's caregivers. There is also acknowledgement of the importance of proper management of grief when dealing with clients presenting with issues surrounding loss. The relationship established by early caregivers/parents opens up awareness of the development of trust and a sense of self-efficacy in the infant. Lack of this healthy development allows for the likelihood of maladaptive and pathological cognitive and emotional ways of functioning to occur.

Two appendices provide the specific instructions and steps to using her techniques in psychotherapy. This material provides a blueprint for this psychotherapeutic work.

In utilizing snippets from her interactions in her clients' therapy sessions as well as pieces from her personal and family history, Dr. Wilson has written a very readable and educational treatise on work with clients who present in our offices with a desire to better understand and change their life trajectory. I would highly recommend this book for any beginning, intermediate, and advanced professional who is involved with the psychotherapeutic journey of clients seeking change in their lives.

Jim Eliuk, Ph. D., R. Psych (AB)
Clinical Supervisor (Ret.)
Department of Educational Psychology,.
University of Alberta

Preface

At the age of 15, after helping my younger sister resolve an issue with her boyfriend, I decided then and there that I liked how that felt and I would become a psychiatrist in order to do psychotherapy. Without ever checking out other options, I set my sights on medical school. With exposure to the theoretical focus of what was being taught about psychiatry in that medical school, I became soured to the thought of becoming a psychiatrist and changed my focus to a residency in Family Medicine post graduation.

During that program, I had a very challenging patient in the family medicine practice and in spite of the option of having my supervisor view my work with this woman via a one-way mirror, he never did. When I asked him why, he told me that he disliked her and I did a better job with her than he could. One day, a visiting psychiatrist came through the clinic. After discussing this patient with the visitor, my supervisor gave me a sheet of paper describing what this psychiatrist believed was the diagnosis for this patient: Munchausen's syndrome! As I read through the description of this disorder I became progressively more annoyed. I told my supervisor that is was all very well that this document told me what was wrong with her but it did not tell me what to do with her!

Many psychiatric diagnoses do this. They lump together a group of symptoms and call them a disorder without offering much in the way of explaining cause or treatment. If you were to go to the emergency department with chest pain, the doctors there would make a determined effort to specify cause so as to provide the appropriate treatment. They would not just give you a pain pill! Unfortunately, someone diagnosed with anxiety is given anti-anxiety medication. Psychotherapy might be recommended along with the medication, provided by someone other than the psychiatrist.

Fortunately, it was very serendipitous that the program I attended also facilitated residents doing outpatient psychotherapy with guidance from the faculty psychiatrists who had developed the McMaster Model of family therapy. I got back on track with an approach that made sense to me. This Systems therapy approach looked at people in context and offered options for change that did not involve medication. As well, it allowed me to adopt an approach to psychological ill health that was based on symptoms, and symptom resolution, not labels that would limit an individual's potential.

Eventually I did more graduate level training in marital and family therapy and in June of 1987 I took the step of leaving family practice and limiting my work to psychotherapy. Finally I was doing the work I had always wanted to do. I continued with graduate coursework, clinical practicums and professional supervision to ensure that I had a good grounding in this new endeavor. A few years later my clinical consultant and mentor, Dr. Allen Vanderwell, introduced me to the work of Milton Erickson. That had a big impact on my appreciation for the use of hypnosis in therapy. Erickson's fundamental attitude of respect for the unconscious and the innate resourcefulness of people, as well as an understanding of the naturalistic nature of trance experiences, rang true for me. This exposure profoundly influenced my work for the remainder of my professional career.

I was asked at times if I would become depressed, knowing all that I knew of the worst of people in hearing the stories of trauma experienced by my clients. I did not. I regularly came away from a day in my office with a sense of amazement that the individuals I worked with had the ability to hang on to the best in themselves in spite of what had been done to them. They challenged me to be the best resource I could be in their healing endeavors.

I retired from clinical practice in June of 2019 and have now had the time to put what I have learned, created, and taught in many conference workshops, into the form of a book that will be accessible to all clinical therapists looking for more options in the treatment of trauma. Thank you for your interest.

Marie A. Wilson,
M.D.

Table of Contents

Introduction - Updating the Indelible 1

The Biologic Pathway to Trauma Memory Resolution..............7

Research Protocols for Trauma Memory Resolution 21

The Re-Definition of Self Process...28

Secure Attachment, Efficacy and Resilience............................65

Grief Work 80

Simplified practice version of the RDS Process......................91

Grief Work Letter Writing Exercise 95

Introduction - Updating the Indelible

An incessant problem in the practice of psychotherapy is the difficulty therapists encounter in attempting to resolve the psychological after effects of trauma. As recently as 1989, LeDoux referred to these effects as "indelible and cognitively impenetrable emotional associations" (LeDoux, Romanski, & Xagoraris, p.241). If this was the conclusion of a biological researcher at that time, it is not surprising that his conclusions reflected the experiences of clinical psychotherapists. Why are the psychological effects of trauma so hard to resolve? The simple answer is that fear-based learning is meant to be permanent. It is about survival. Humans, like other species, have evolved to become very efficient in recognizing danger and in rapidly and permanently retaining that learning. We establish physical and emotional strategies to protect ourselves. The instinctual responses to danger of fighting, fleeing, or freezing may have some effectiveness in the context in which they are learned. If our strategies are effective, we feel empowered. If not, we remain afraid.

Children are born entirely dependent on those around them. They are physically unable to provide for their own basic needs of food, shelter, and clothing, needs made necessary by a will to live. Amazingly, in spite of their extreme vulnerability and innate fears of falling and asphyxiation, most are not born with other fears. Babies are not afraid to cry, the primary tool available to them, to trigger interaction with the external world. Fortunately, for most babies that signal will result in an appropriately caring response. Their needs will be met.

A response that is not appropriate will trigger fear, the awareness that the attempts to communicate have failed. Other strategies may then be employed. If these additional attempts result in a corrective response, the fear will be assuaged. My one-year-old son was very upset with me after the first time he was away from me for more than a night. He refused to be held or comforted. I have often advised others to look for the message behind the behavior and I did this with him. As I spoke what I felt might be his distress over feeling abandoned by me, and validated his dislike of what had happened, he settled. Being validated in our distress reinforces a sense of trust in our own awareness and our abilities to use that awareness to take care of ourselves. At the age of three, my daughter displayed this self-trust. Crying after a fall, her grandmother helped her up and told her to stop crying because it didn't hurt anymore. My daughter responded by questioning, "How do you know? It's not your body." She didn't doubt her own knowing.

Fear inducing experiences, where a child is unable to advocate for themselves to initiate validation or repair, will result in a sense of powerlessness. Self-trust is disrupted as the repeated failures undermine efficacy. Being dependent on others for their survival, and as they progressively distrust their own internal guidance system of feelings and perceptions, they turn to those others for certainty. They will come to accept the belief that they are responsible for the harm they endure because that is what they are told. They need to believe that the people who are responsible for their survival know what they are doing. They have no other choice.

Our personal security rests in our ability to effectively respond to what comes our way. This is the only authority we truly have. Everything else is outside of us. When a dependent child is denied any direct control over their survival, this will give rise to additional, fear-induced survival strategies as they try to control the world outside of them. Behaviors emerge that reflect these attempts at control. Some of these include: passive avoidance of conflict, people pleasing, silencing of complaint, vigilant observation of the behavior of others in an attempt to predict risk, defensive anger, lying, and bullying. They have some survival value but do not result in the certainty of emotional security. These strategies appear very early on in a child's development and their origin may become part of their implicit memory. The adult they become may have no conscious recall of their initiation.

The necessity and appropriateness of these survival strategies, created in the primary context, is often lost over time. With the physical independence of adulthood, these survival strategies will have outlived their usefulness. Unfortunately, as part of the permanent fear-induced learning that is held implicitly, the responses remain intact and are automatically expressed beyond conscious control. The contextual aspects, the sights, sounds, and physical feelings associated with the initial fear-based learning experience, become the triggers for their expression.

Ongoing life experiences, consciously recalled traumas, will reinforce their intensity. These survival strategies are then labeled as pathological symptoms as they become more generalized and severely maladaptive. This is the underlying issue in all of the trauma induced psychological symptoms that people complain of post-traumatically. For example, someone repeatedly mistreated during childhood might learn to limit their expression of distress in order to avoid further injury. As an adult, submission to an abusive spouse would replicate the response to that initial intimidation. Even thinking about the abusive partner would trigger emotional distress and a repeated experience of powerlessness. This powerlessness is usually incongruent with the resourcefulness of the individual in their adult life. The logical, conscious awareness of this incongruence is not enough to change the automatic, unconsciously generated response.

People have lived with the consequences of trauma, both physically and psychologically, since we emerged as a species. The respectful acceptance of the existence of the symptomatic presentation of what psychological trauma looks like has only come to the forefront in general awareness since the Vietnam War. Post Traumatic Stress Disorder, PTSD, is a label used in common parlance for any collection of symptoms someone might have post-trauma. The descriptions, criteria, and definitions of what constitutes PTSD, or other trauma-based diagnoses, keep evolving. In parallel, many trauma therapy treatment approaches have emerged. These have had varying degrees of popularity and success.

Understanding how a problem began is useful, but rarely changes the current experience of the person being treated. Logical explanations do little to resolve emotional suffering. Referring to victims as survivors, when anyone still breathing is surviving, minimizes the courage demonstrated by those willing to face the turmoil of their lives. Those who come out the other side of trauma and make a determined effort to heal themselves are doing much more than just surviving. They are people who have maintained their humanity in spite of the potential for the trauma to dehumanize them. When clients seek therapy, they have already been coping with their symptoms. Therapeutic efforts, aimed at helping them cope better, deny the possibility that they have the potential to thrive, free of those hindrances.

I am much more interested in helping people to thrive. My clients have always inspired me and this kept me going in my practice as a trauma therapist. The desire to be an effective therapist and to honor my clients' trust pushed me to keep searching and exposing myself to many theoretical and practical therapy approaches over my career. It challenged me to be creative. There have been many respected mentors along the way as well as others for whom I felt nothing but disdain.

One conference presenter, who confused resignation with the Buddhist concept of acceptance, approached his torture victim clients with an attitude of luck-of-the-draw fatalism. You may not have any control over what is done to you; you will always have the option to do something about the aftermath. People are victimized but remaining a victim is optional.

So how do we update fear memories and resolve the emotional sequelae of trauma? How do we help people move from coping to thriving? Biological research with animal models has provided me with an understanding of what is necessary to accomplish this end. Those stubborn, fear-based memories can be updated and, as it turns out, fear memories are not indelible. In the first chapter I will review this research, and the conclusions that I have drawn from it, that outline a pathway for updating fear memories and resolving symptomatology.

This pathway can be used as a substrate to evaluate the potential effectiveness of various trauma therapy protocols. In chapter two I will review a sampling of published research protocols whose effectiveness may be explained by this biological pathway. In the third chapter I will present a detailed description of the protocol I have developed, the Re-definition of Self Process. From its beginnings in 1992, it has evolved over time to become a very effective tool for use in resolving the trauma symptoms of my clients. I will highlight the elements of this biological pathway in its structure, information that has told me why the protocol is effective.

In chapter four, in a review of Attachment Theory Research, I will expand on the influence of early learning experiences that I have described earlier in this introduction. A sense of personal efficacy is necessary in order to trust that you have the ability to figure things out and to bounce back from adversity. The research demonstrates how efficacy is established or undermined very early in life and explains why some people are more resilient than others. Those people who respond very poorly to traumatic events have often been primed by early life experiences. The new events reinforce their existing sense of powerlessness.

Finally, I will end the book with a chapter on the topic of grief, that underappreciated and absolutely essential emotion that allows us to say goodbye to what no longer is and to move on to new beginnings. Effective grieving is an essential part of trauma resolution as well as a part of dealing with everyday losses, big and small.

Reference

LeDoux, J., Romanski, L., & Xagoraris, A. (1989). Indelibility of subcortical emotional memories. *Journal of Cognitive Neuroscience*, 1, 238-243.

CHAPTER ONE

The Biologic Pathway to Trauma Memory Resolution

In order to explain the biological process required for the resolution of trauma memories, it is important to define the terminology used in the description of the research.

The first terms that need to be defined are those related to memory formation and modification. More than a hundred years ago, researchers concluded "a memory trace was formed gradually over time after acquisition" (Sara, 2006, p. 515). This process of gradual formation is referred to as *consolidation* and requires protein synthesis to make the memory trace (Nader, Schafe, & LeDoux, 2000, p. 722). With any sensory perception of exposure to the contextual triggers that were part of the learning experience, memories are *activated*. These triggers may be very subtle (Hupbach, Gomez, Hardt & Nadel, 2007, p. 52). Even a vague sense of familiarity is activating a memory, although we may not have conscious awareness at that moment of what that familiarity is associated with. The underlying memory will still have been activated.

Once a memory has been activated, it may be *retrieved*. Many authors use the words activation and retrieval interchangeably. I understand them to define separate experiences. Activation wakes up a memory, priming it (Sara, 2000, p. 75). Retrieval is the conscious recall of the memory. Memories may frequently be modified without conscious retrieval of the original learning. For example, I have no recollection of how I learned to walk or how I modified my gait after taking ballet classes. I do recall consciously correcting my gait and the persistent effort it took to do so. I no longer have to pay attention to my gait as the newest version of that learned memory is the automatic one now.

The use of our memory would become exhausting if we had to consciously retrieve all the memories of acquisition. We want to have our memory work for us beyond conscious awareness. A well known example of having to consciously reactivate memory is the experience of Milton Erickson. In 1918, at the age of seventeen, he was paralyzed with polio, only able to hear, move his eyes, and speak with difficulty. He had no other conscious control over his body. Over the next two years, he facilitated his own recovery.

> Milton foraged through his sense memories to try to relearn how to move. He would stare for hours at his hand, for example, and try to recall how his fingers had felt when grasping a pitchfork. Bit by bit he found his fingers beginning to twitch and move in tiny, uncoordinated ways. He persisted until the movements became larger and until he could consciously control them (Erickson, 1983, p.12).

Gradually, he recovered full mobility and went on to become a renowned psychiatrist. He used his own experiences in the development of the theories and practice of naturalistic hypnosis, what is commonly known as Ericksonian Hypnosis.

The activation of a memory makes it *labile*, or destabilized, and open to modification. This lability is not diminished by the passage of time since creation of the memory trace (Sara, 2006, p. 516). New memories are "made upon the background of prior experience [and] . . . cannot be acquired independently of retrieval of past experience, in that it is memory of the past which organizes and provides meaning to the present perceptual experience" (Sara, 2006, p. 519). Additional protein synthesis is required for the new information to modify and update the original memory trace (Hupbach, et al., 2007, p. 47). This newly modified memory trace is then *reconsolidated* (Debiec & LeDoux, 2004, p. 811). This term has caused some debate in the research community with Sara saying, "Every consolidation is, in fact, a 'reconsolidation'" (2006, p. 519). Rodriquez-Ortiz and Bermudez-Rattoni (2007) disagree. They have attempted further clarification of this process in their research and have come up with another term: *updated consolidation*. Updated consolidation refers to activated memory that is "modified by the integration of updated relevant experience" (section 11.6) versus simple reinforcement and reconsolidation of the same information.

For example, if I am learning to play the piano I will do a lesson and practice the new skills. With a first exposure to this new skill, I will create and consolidate a memory trace. (The learning to play may be new, but I will have seen or heard a piano played previously.) The next day, the act of sitting down to the piano again (a contextual trigger), will immediately cause activation and probable conscious retrieval of the previously learned memory trace. The lability of this trace will allow for its modification. New pieces of relevant information added (via protein synthesis) to the original memory trace will result in an updated consolidation.

Research suggests that there is a limited period of time for this to occur. The window of opportunity to add new information to a memory trace begins by ten minutes after memory activation and ends within a six-hour time frame (Schiller, et al., 2010, p. 50). Once an updated consolidation has occurred, the memory returns to a stable state. Sara has also reported that memory can be reactivated during the period of rapid eye movement (REM), dream state sleep (2006, p. 518). This reactivation results in a reinforced reconsolidation that is demonstrated by a strengthening of the original learning acquired during the waking state.

Unfortunately this is also true for fear memories, as "REM sleep seems to benefit particularly memory that is not dependent on cortico-hippocampal circuitry, including procedural skills, object recognition memory and amygdala-mediated cued fear conditioning" (Dudai, Karni & Born, 2015, p. 24). Sleeping after experiencing a trauma event may strengthen the fear memory that was created.

Memories of the non-fearful stories of our lives are created and stored separately from fear-based memories. Non-threatening or declarative memories are generally created and stored in the hippocampus of the brain (Bechara, et al., 1995; Phelps, 2004). This is not the case for fear-based memories.

> It does not matter what kind of stimulus you use to turn the amygdala on, it does not matter what kind of response you measure as fear response, and it does not matter what kind of animal you do the experiment on, as long as that animal has as amygdala, the amygdala is involved in fear processing (Debiec & LeDoux, 2004, p. 810).

As I said before, fear-based learning is meant to be permanent. Initially, like non-threatening memories, the fear memory is consolidated soon after the event. Re-exposure to the contextual triggers of the traumatic experience, be it auditory, visual, olfactory, gustatory, or kinesthetic, will activate the memory *but will not automatically labilize, or destabilize, the initial memory structure to allow for updating that would change the meaning of the original trace* (Pedreira, Pérez-Cuesta & Maldonado, 2010, p. 581).

Instead, this re-exposure may induce a surge of stress hormones that will reinforce the original learning, a reconsolidation that says things are even worse than what was felt before (Debiec, Bush & LeDoux, 2011, p. 186). As well, the amygdala and hippocampus respond differently to the effects of stress hormones. With chronic stress, the amygdala will get larger while the hippocampus will get smaller, losing neuronal connections

(Sapolsky, Uno, Rebert & Finch, 1990, p. 2897; Vyas, Mitra, Rao & Chattarji, 2002, p. 6815). Chronic stress could result in a loss of hippocampal inhibitory control while exacerbating the excitatory control of the amygdala (Vyas et al., 2002, p. 6817). "These findings may account for several behavioral manifestations. Individuals who suffered from severe traumatic experiences can sometimes develop amnesia for the event but at the same time they may have enhanced emotional responsiveness to the trauma-related stimuli" (Debiec & LeDoux, 2004, p. 812).

I have referred to contextual triggers, internal or external incoming information, in the description above, and more clarification of what those are and how they work is needed here. An *Unconditioned Stimulus (US)* is something that naturally and automatically triggers a response. For example, the firing of a gun aimed towards you would be a danger stimulus, an US.

A danger stimulus triggers the release of stress hormones that induce internal physiological changes such as muscle tension, increased heart rate, nausea, sweating, and changes in breathing - all reactions preceding freeze, fight or flight responses. These physiological changes become internal, endogenous, contextual stimuli. Add to this the external, exogenous, contextual signals perceived through one's senses (the image of the assailant; the noise of the shot; the smell of gun powder) and these all become *Conditioned Stimuli (CS)*. They are pieces of the learning context.

In future, these endogenous and exogenous conditioned stimuli have the potential to elicit a fear response without the presence of any defined danger. These are learned responses that occur by association and can be established via a single learning event, such as what occurred with one of my cats. She was taken to the veterinarian to have a microchip placed under her skin and this was done without anesthesia and with the use of a large bore needle. It was probably a painful experience for her. She was then placed in her carrier to come home. From then on, she could only be placed in the carrier when sedated, as she would resist, tooth and claw, if not medicated. The carrier, as part of the learning context, was associated with the painful experience.

The next term that requires definition is the word *Extinction*. Extinction is a gradual weakening of a conditioned response that results in the behavior decreasing or disappearing over time. This can occur when there is continuous exposure to the conditioned stimuli, the learning context, without the presentation of the danger, the unconditioned stimulus (Pedreira, et al., 2004, p. 583). Perhaps if I had left the open cat carrier in her space at all times, my cat would gradually have not reacted to it.

Inadvertently, I reinforced her reactivity by only bringing out the carrier when it was needed. Intermittent exposure to the CS can strengthen the response and make it more difficult to extinguish. As well, extinguishing a response to a conditioned stimulus does not cause a return to an unconditioned state because extinction only forms a "new memory that hinders the expression of the old one" (Pedreira, et al., 2004, p. 581). As well, expression of the fear memory response can be re-established with re-exposure to the danger signal, the unconditioned stimulus (Kindt, Soeter & Vervliet, 2009, para. 6).

The former soldier who drops to the ground after hearing the retort of a car misfiring is doing what his memory tells him he must do to survive a danger. Of course it doesn't make sense in his current context. He could go through extinction training to consciously learn to tolerate these noises and progressively create a new memory that is not associated with a fearful response. Provided with another aversive stimulus though, such as someone pointing a gun at him, his reactivity will return to its original intensity. That original memory remains intact. "Behavioral extinction of emotional responses may represent a temporary suppression, by cortex, of subcortical (thalamo-amygdala) emotional circuits that maintain the learned association over long, perhaps indefinite, periods of time" (LeDoux, Romanski & Xagoraris, 1989, p. 241).

With this background of information, I will go on to describe the biological pathway for the resolution of trauma memories. I use the word pathway to imply a process of movement from one point to another. The beginning point in this description is the stable memory trace that has previously been consolidated.

1. Activation

The first step along this pathway is activation of the stable memory. The context re-exposure can include exogenous environmental cues, the conditioned sensory stimuli. As well, the endogenous, physiological state of the individual provides an internal contextual reminder of the learning. This internal state is mediated by the release of stress hormones that increase arousal. It is a common human experience to have an environmental cue such as a loud noise, a particular odor, or an angry expression act as a trigger to the internal release of corticosteroid stress hormones that recreate an internal context of hyperarousal. Any client, in any therapy office, who describes some emotional distress triggered by a recent event, (especially when they recognize that their distress is out of proportion to the actual threat of that event), is activating a memory.

2. Retrieval

Once activated, memory retrieval needs to be facilitated. In lab animals, the researchers who have done the training easily verify evidence of memory retrieval. Memory retrieval for people is much more complex. When individuals have conscious recall of a specific traumatic experience, the detailed narrative of the memory can be readily accessed. What becomes more difficult for people is the fear-based learning that is held unconsciously either as implicit or dissociated memory. In spite of the controversy surrounding the use of hypnosis for memory retrieval, hypnosis "represents one of the oldest and possibly one of the most effective ways of helping people revisit past trauma" (Turner, McFarlane & van der Kolk, 1996, p. 548). Regardless of how the retrieval occurs, it is a necessary step in the progress towards fear memory resolution in people.

3. Labilization

The next step on this pathway is the labilization, or desta-bilization of the original memory. It must become labile for new learning to structurally modify the original fear memory trace. Non fear-based memories become labile when activated, whereas fear memory labilization is more restricted because this kind of learning is meant to be permanent.

Fear-based learning tries to protect us from harm by offering us predictions about what will come next. When there is a mismatch of expectations, because the predictions about reality are not confirmed in current experience, labilization of fear memory occurs. Two conditions are required to create this mismatch: a termination of the learning context cues within a six hour time window (the conditioned stimuli), and a lack of re-inforcement of the aversive unconditioned stimulus (Pedreira, et al., 2004, p.583). A client, who describes a distressing event while in a therapist's office, will not have sustained exposure to the contextual triggers (the CS). The physiological arousal associated with the oral report will settle in a supportive and safe envi-ronment. Ideally, the client will not leave the session still upset. As well, they will not experience any threat to their safety (the US). Under these conditions, the inaccuracy of the memory's prediction will make the fear memory trace labile.

The "memory repair mechanism would not entail an obligatory phase of every retrieved memory but a mechanism of exception" (Pedreira, et al., 2004, p. 583) triggered by the mismatch. Ongoing conditioned stimuli, for a period of time beyond the six-hour time limit needed for reconsolidation, will not cause labilization of the memory even when there is no aversive stimulus. Instead of labilization, the memory would be extinguished. A new memory would be created but the old fear memory would still exist unexpressed (Pedreira, et al., 2004, p. 583).

4. Updating

Any emotionally and physically safe psychotherapeutic context can provide the conditions for labilization of fear memories. It is during this period of labilization that it is possible to update the original memory. *Effective updating is the crucial element in trauma memory resolution.*

Unfortunately, it is very common for people to revisit trauma memories repeatedly without experiencing any emotional resolution. Instead, they may feel worse. As confirmed by the research of Sara, "a high level of attention and arousal at the time of retrieval will play a capital role in reinforcing the memory, since neuromodulatory systems are activated during these behavioral states" (2000, p. 81). Emotional arousal and a surge in stress hormones will occur with the opening of old wounds. The empathic witnessing of the oral narrative by the therapist will not change the meaning attached to the memory if the individual continues to view himself or herself as a powerless victim of the past experience.

The client knowing they were not safe or cared about in the past readily counters a therapist telling a client that they are safe and cared about currently. *Current life experience of the client is irrelevant if it is not used to change the meaning ascribed to the events of the past.* It is not a safe bet to believe that the more you talk about the trauma, the less problematic it will become. There may be some extinction with prolonged exposure to the story of the trauma, but therapy sessions don't go on for more than six hours at a time. These are common therapeutic approaches that may reinforce the original trauma memory as opposed to updating the memory.

Updating must include new and experientially relevant information in reference to the past traumatic memory for the fear memory to be modified. "Updating does not imply erasing of previous learning but incorporation of a related learning" (Rodriguez-Ortiz & Bermudez-Rattoni, 2007, section 11.6). Learning that changes the individual's perception of themselves, *in relation to the past experience,* will update the fear memory. *When an individual who is looking back on a past experience is able to perceive themselves as resourceful, versus helpless, that new information removes the elements of fear and powerlessness that have persisted over time.*

In my work with clients I suggested that the memory was a small snapshot of the events in the past. By filling in the missing elements and expanding the view, the image became much larger and impossible to shrink down to the original picture. That fear memory will have been changed. In the next chapter, I will describe how removing the element of fear is accomplished in the updating done in various trauma therapy research protocols. These have been proven to be effective. As well, in chapter three that describes the protocol I have developed, I will describe how I accomplish this updating of removing the element of fear *as well as of filling in the missing parts of the picture, all the resourcefulness not previously owned by the client.*

5. Updated Consolidation

Again, the process of incorporating new information into the old memory trace requires protein synthesis in the amygdala. This occurs during a limited period of time, from ten minutes to six hours after retrieval (Schiller, et al., 2010, p. 50), and is necessary if a memory is to persist (Nader, et al., 2000, p. 723). Once this time window has closed, the updated memory becomes stable as an updated consolidation. What is important here is that the synthesis of protein is a fundamental biological process that changes the physical structure of the original fear memory trace.

The retrieved fear memory no longer exists in its original form and therefore cannot be reactivated by the previous contextual triggers that have been dealt with. This has been clearly demonstrated in the long-term follow-up of human research subjects (Schiller, et al., 2009; Brunet, et al., 2011). The description of this research will be included in the next chapter, in the review of effective therapy protocols that incorporate this pathway. This is a very different outcome than what occurs with extinction training where a new memory competes for expression with the intact fear memory, which can be reactivated (Schiller, et al., 2009 p. 51; Kindt, et al., 2009, para. 6; Duvarci, & Nader, 2004, p. 9271).

Along with the stabilization that occurs with this initial six hour updated consolidation process, an "enhancement phase of consolidation requires sleep" (Walker, Brakefield, Hobson & Stickgold, 2003, p. 617), particularly during REM sleep for the amygdala mediated affective part of the memory and during slow wave sleep for the hippocampal, declarative and behavioural memory, component (Sara, 2000, p. 79).

In summary, these are the five steps of the biological and emotional pathway that I have concluded as being necessary for fear memory updating and resolution: activation, retrieval, labilization, updating, and updated consolidation. I haven't found the description of this pathway specified previously, although I expect it underlies the research that has been done.

A personal and simple example of this pathway in action goes back to the experience of my cat. At age thirteen, she became very ill. On a very cold January morning I medicated her to take her to the vet in her carrier. She underwent some tests and while waiting for the results, she stayed warm lying on a warming pad in the open carrier and comforted as I stroked her. She needed to go back to the vet clinic the next day and I left the open carrier in her space at home. That evening, she voluntarily used the carrier as a place to sleep. This was a completely unexpected new behavior and I can only assume that she had updated her fear memory associated with the carrier to now link it with comfort versus pain.

Her resistance to being placed in the carrier never returned even with the ongoing need for many trips to the vet. As well, if the effect was solely that of extinction, I would have expected a return of the fear reaction because, over the last few years of her life, she was repeatedly supplemented with fluids supplied under her skin via the use of a large bore needle! Neither this aversive stimulus of the needle use nor the contextual trigger of the carrier ever elicited the previous fear response from her. I can only assume that the fear memory was fundamentally altered; that an updated consolidation had occurred. This was the only longitudinal "animal research" that I had any experience with. Fortunately, I have had many more experiences of witnessing the resolution of trauma with my clients in over thirty years of practice as a psychotherapist. I will describe what has come of that work in chapter three.

References

Bechara, A., Tranel, D., Damasio, H., Adolphs, R., Rockland, C., & Damasio, A.R. (1995). Double dissociation of conditioning and declarative knowledge relative to the amygdala and hippocampus in humans. *Science, 269*, 1115-1118.

Brunet, A., Poundja, J., Tremblay, J., Bui, E., Thomas, E., Orr, S. P., Azzoug, A., Birmes, P., & Pitman, R. K. (2011). Trauma reactivation under the influence of propranolol decreases posttraumatic stress symptoms and disorder 3 open-label trials. *Journal of Clinical Psychopharmacology, 31(4)*, 547-550.

Debiec, J., & LeDoux, J. E. (2004). Fear and the brain. *Social Research, 71(4)*, 807-818.

Debiec, J., Bush, D. E. A., & LeDoux, J. E. (2011). Noradrenergic enhancement of reconsolidation in the amygdala impairs extinction of conditioned fear in rats – a possible mechanism for the persistence of traumatic memories in PTSD. *Depression and Anxiety, (28)*, 186-193.

Dudai, Y., Karni, A., Born, J. (2015). The consolidation and transformation of memory. *Neuron, 88, (1)*, 20-32.

Duvarci, S., & Nader, K. (2004). Characterization of fear memory reconsolidation. *The Journal of Neuroscience, 24(42)*, 9269-9275.

Erickson, M., H. (1983). *Healing in Hypnosis: The seminars, workshops, and lectures of Milton H. Erickson, volume 1* (E. L. Rossi, M. O. Ryan & F. A. Sharp, Eds.). New York: Irvington.

Hupbach, A., Gomez, R., Hardt, O., & Nadel, L. (2007). Reconsolidation of episodic memories: A subtle reminder triggers integration of new information. *Learning and Memory, 14(1-2)*, 47-53.

Kindt, M., Soeter, M., & Vervliet, B. (2009). Beyond extinction: erasing human fear responses and preventing the return of fear. *Nature Neuroscience, 12*, 256-258. doi:10.1038/nn.2271

LeDoux, J., Romanski, L., & Xagoraris, A. (1989). Indelibility of subcortical emotional memories. *Journal of Cognitive Neuroscience, 1*, 238-243.

Nader, K., Schafe, G. E., & Le Doux, J. E. (2000). Fear memories require protein synthesis in the amygdala for reconsolidation after retrieval. *Nature, 406*, 722-726.

Pedreira, M. E., Pérez-Cuesta, L. M., & Maldonado, H. (2004). Mismatch between what is expected and what actually occurs triggers memory reconsolidation or extinction. *Cold Spring Harbor Laboratory Press, 11*, 579-585. http://www.learnmem.org/cgi/doi/10.1101/lm.76904.

Phelps, E. A. (2004). Human emotion and memory: Interactions of the amygdala and hippocampal complex. *Current Opinion in Neurobiology, 14*, 198-202.

Rodriguez-Ortiz C. J., & Bermúdez-Rattoni, F. (2007). Memory Reconsolidation or Updating Consolidation? In: Bermúdez-Rattoni, F. (Editor). *Neural Plasticity and Memory: From Genes to Brain Imaging.* (Chapter 11). Boca Raton (FL): CRC Press/Taylor & Francis. Available from: https://www.ncbi.nlm.nih.gov/books/NBK3905/

Sapolsky, R. M., Uno, H., Rebert, C. S., & Finch, C.E. (1990). Hippocampal damage associated with prolonged glucocorticoids exposure in primates. *The Journal of Neuroscience, 10(9)*, 2897-2902.

Sara, S. J. (2000). Retrieval and reconsolidation: Toward a neurobiology of remembering. *Learning & Memory, 7*, 73-84.

Sara, S. J., & Hars, B. (2006). In memory of consolidation. *Learning & Memory, 13*, 515-521.

Schiller, D., Monfils, M. H., Raio, C. M., Johnson, D. C., LeDoux, J. E., & Phelps, E. A. (2010). Preventing the return of fear in humans using reconsolidation update mechanisms. *Nature, 463*, 49-53. doi:10.1038/nature08637.

Turner, S. W., McFarlane, A. C., & van der Kolk, B. A. (1996). The thera-peutic environment and new explorations in the treatment of posttraumatic stress disorder. In B. A. van der Kolk, A. C. McFarlane, & L. Weisaeth (Eds.). *Traumatic stress: The effects of overwhelming experience on mind, body, and society.* (p. 537-558). New York: Guilford Press.

Walker, M. P., Brakefield, T., Hobson, J. A., & Stickgold, R. (2003). Dissociable stages of human memory consolidation and reconsolidation. *Nature 425,* 616-620. doi:10.1038/nature01951.

Vyas, A., Mitra, R., Shankaranarayana Rao. B. S., & Chattarji, S. (2002). Chronic stress induces contrasting patterns of dendritic remodelling in hippocampal and amygdaloid neurons. *The Journal of Neuroscience, 22(15),* 6810-6818.

CHAPTER TWO

Research Protocols for Trauma Memory Resolution

In this chapter, I will review research protocols that have been used with human subjects. In their structure, these protocols exemplify the elements of the trauma resolution pathway described in chapter one. Up to this point, much of the information that I have referenced has been gleaned from animal research. With animal research, it is possible to use drugs, enzymes, and neurotransmitters (naturally occurring chemicals in the body) that are injected directly into the brains of the animals in order to assess their impact on trauma memory consolidation and updated consolidation. This isn't an option with people. One of the drugs that can be given orally to people is the drug propranolol.

Propranolol has been an approved medication for use in people since the 1960's with its initial use being in the treatment of high blood pressure. This drug is a beta-blocker, a beta-adrenergic antagonist, meaning that it will block receptors in the brain, heart, and lungs that would normally be available to receive the stimulation of stress neurotransmitters such as epinephrine (also referred to as adrenaline). As a result, propranolol will reduce the emotional and physiological experiences of anxiety, (fear, rapid heart rate, rapid breathing, nausea, sweating, and raised blood pressure) in moments that would otherwise be felt to be stressful. When this drug was injected directly into the amygdala of research animals and interfered with the reconsolidation of fear memories, it was suggested that there was a "beta-receptor-dependent phase" during reconsolidation (Sara, 2000, p 80).

In a double blind study, Pitman and colleagues identified the effectiveness of using propranolol to reduce physiological responses to later recall of a trauma if the drug was given shortly after the occurrence of that trauma and during the time window for consolidation of the initial trauma memory (Pitman, et al, 2002). This study led to further research by members of this group to investigate the effects of giving propranolol to subjects with verified, chronic posttraumatic stress disorder (Brunet & Orr, et al., 2008).

Nineteen subjects completed two standardized script preparation forms describing different aspects of their consciously remembered trauma event. Understandably, this effort triggered trauma symptomatology for the subjects. Nine people were then given propranolol and ten were given placebo in the same double blind dosing regimen.

One week later these subjects listened to a thirty second summary of each of their trauma descriptions and then spent another thirty seconds re-imagining the trauma experience. Their consequent physiological arousal was measured via heart rate, skin conductance, facial frowning, and electromyography changes. The propranolol treated group experienced significantly less physiological arousal than did the placebo group.

These researchers wanted to find out if the improvements in symptomatology could be enhanced by repeated treatment sessions and if the results would be sustained over time. The next study (Brunet & Poundja, et al., 2011) included a pretreatment assessment, six treatment sessions at weekly intervals, and a follow up session six months later. Three study groups in different locations, who all had clinically defined PTSD, were included in this research. All test subjects were given a dose of propranolol in advance of providing an account of their trauma event.

In subsequent sessions, after being given propranolol ninety minutes earlier, each subject read aloud their recorded story and was asked to revivify the memory while doing so. These sessions were time limited in order to prevent the possibility of extinction with prolonged exposure to the triggering stimuli. There was a progressive and significant reduction in all of the PTSD symptoms for the subjects treated with propranolol, compared to the control group, with sustained and even further reduction in symptoms at six months follow-up.

An enhancement of this protocol was used in further research (Poundja, Sanche, Tremblay, & Brunet, 2012) to assess the impact of this approach for trauma resolution on co-morbid issues: symptoms not directly related to PTSD; negative emotions; and, overall quality of life. The researchers also wanted to assess the deterrent effect of: sociodemographic variables (age, gender); trauma related variables (duration, type of trauma); and, psychiatric co- morbidity (depression, borderline personality disorders), in undermining the effectiveness of this therapy approach. The participants were asked to be very detailed in their descriptions of the trauma event that resulted in PTSD; all the contextual, emotional, sensory, and physiological details, that they could recall. During the subsequent treatment sessions, the oral narrative was expanded upon.

The interviewer asked questions that facilitated a sustained focus and elicited more information about the past and present feelings. Changes noticed since the previous session were also identified. The treatment subjects experienced a reduction in PTSD symptomatology, negative emotions, and co-morbid symptoms. Quality of life improved as well. The only variable that was significant in limiting the effectiveness of this approach was gender based; women experienced a greater degree of improvement than did men. The authors did not explain the purpose for the intensification of the narrative portion of their protocol.

Kindt, Soeter, and Vervliet, (2009), conducted their own research into the effectiveness of propranolol use to resolve a fear memory. Using an unconditioned stimulus of mild electric shock along with conditioned stimuli such as pictures of spiders, a reliable fear reaction was established. This research concluded, yet again, that "one reactivation trial combined with the administration of propranolol completely eliminated the behavioral expression of the fear memory 24 hours later" (para. 8).

This was a double blind, controlled experiment with different study groups. Consistent with the research of others, exposure to the aversive stimulus in the extinction-trained group did reinstate the fear response. As well, the use of propranolol without activation of the fear memory did not alter the fear response, leading to the conclusion that propranolol acted by disrupting the reconsolidation of the fear response (para. 9).

It was also concluded that "propranolol eliminated the fear response, without affecting declarative memory" (para. 8), meaning that the individual could remember what had caused them to feel afraid previously, without feeling afraid presently. *This is an important conclusion as it is telling us that it is not necessary to erase memory in order to resolve the fear associated with it.* As well, the authors of these five studies all agreed with the hypothesis that propranolol biologically altered the reconsolidation of the fear memory.

A more recent proposal by Gisquet-Verrier and Riccio, and one that I have always thought was more likely, is that the anxiolytic effects of propranolol reduce the emotion connected with the memory. These authors refer to this effect as "emotional remodeling" . . . [where the] . . . "reduced emotional valence could be integrated within the trauma memory, decreasing its negative consequences" (2019, p. 8). *The reduced emotional and physiological effects experienced by a person, who has activated, retrieved, and labilized a trauma memory, will act as the new and relevant information that will update the memory and result in an updated consolidation.* The trauma memory will then be recalled as a fearful event without the individual experiencing the fear and arousal that previously went with it. In that sense, it will become part of their history rather than being experienced anew in the present moment.

The studies that I have discussed so far all included the use of propranolol to effect change in the trauma memory. Schiller and colleagues conducted research to determine if it was possible to interfere with reconsolidation of a fear memory without the use of drugs. They wondered "if an old fear memory could be restored while incorporating neutral or more positive information provided at the time of retrieval" (Schiller, et al., 2010, p. 49).

To do this, they trained three groups of subjects to develop a fear response to a mild shock stimulus (US) associated with the images of two colored squares (CS). Only one of these colored squares had been paired with the shock stimulus. The next day, two groups of subjects had the fear memory reactivated by a single exposure to the CS that had been paired with the shock. One of these groups was reactivated shortly before extinction training. The second group did not undergo extinction training until six hours had passed. This time delay permitted reconsolidation of the trauma memory to occur before the training began. The third group had no reminder of the fear memory before extinction began.

On the third day, it was determined that the subjects, who had experienced extinction training during the period of active memory reconsolidation, (the ten minute to six hour time window), were the only ones to not have a spontaneous re-emergence of the fear response. The fear memory had been updated. This effect was sustained in a one-year follow up assessment.

In a second experiment, they also determined that this resolution of a fear response was cue dependent, meaning that *eliminating the fear response to one associated conditioned stimulus did not automatically eliminate this response to a different conditioned stimulus.* This has relevance in the practice of trauma therapy, as there are many contextual stimuli that are associated with a traumatic event. This may also explain the focus in the research of Poundja (et al., 2012) to include as many of the contextual triggers associated with the target trauma event in the narrative that was used for each subject in the study.

The examples I've described in this chapter are but a sampling of the research protocols that clearly demonstrate how the biological pathway for trauma resolution may be utilized. I have been introduced to many forms of trauma therapy, during conferences and workshops, over my professional life. It has been an interesting exercise to evaluate these options while mindful of this research information. I hope the information I have offered here will encourage others to critically review their own practice, in order to identify this pathway in their own approach or to modify their approach accordingly. I will do just that in the review of my own protocol in the next chapter.

References

Brunet, A., Orr, S. P., Tremblay, J., Robertson, K., Nader, K., & Pitman, R. K. (2008). Effect of post-retrieval propranolol on psychophysiologic responding during subsequent script-driven traumatic imagery in post-traumatic stress disorder. *The Journal of Psychiatric Research*, 43, 503-506. doi:10.1016/j.jpsychires.2007.05.006

Brunet, A., Poundja, J., Tremblay, J., Bui, E., Thomas, E., Orr, S. P., Azzoug, A., Birmes, P., & Pitman, R. K. (2011). Trauma reactivation under the influence of propranolol decreases posttraumatic stress symptoms and disorder 3 open-label trials. *Journal of Clinical Psychopharmacology*, 31(4), 547-550.

Gisquet-Verrier, P. & Riccio, D. C., (2019). Memory integration as a challenge to the consolidation/reconsolidation hypothesis: Similarities, differences and perspectives. *Frontiers in Systems Neuroscience*, 12:71. doi: 10.3389/fnsys.2018.00071

Kindt, M., Soeter, M., & Vervliet, B. (2009). Beyond extinction: erasing human fear responses and preventing the return of fear. *Nature Neuroscience*, 12, 256-258. doi:10.1038/nn.2271

Pitman, R. K., Sanders, K. M., Zusman, R. M., Healy, A. R., Cheema, F., Lasko, N. B., Cahill, L., & Orr, S. P. (2002). Pilot study of secondary prevention of posttraumatic stress disorder with propranolol. *Biological Psychiatry*, 51(2), p. 189-192.

Poundja, J., Sanche, S. Tremblay, J., & Brunet, A. (2012). Trauma reactivation under the influence of propranolol: An examination of clinical predictors. *European Journal of Psychotraumatology*, 3:1, 15470, DOI: 10.3402/ejpt.v3i0,15470.

Sara, S. J. (2000). Retrieval and reconsolidation: Toward a neurobiology of remembering. *Learning & Memory*, 7, 73-84.

Schiller, D., Monfils, M. H., Raio, C. M., Johnson, D. C., LeDoux, J. E., & Phelps, E. A. (2010). Preventing the return of fear in humans using reconsolidation update mechanisms. *Nature*, 463, 49-53. doi:10.1038/nature08637.

CHAPTER THREE

The Re-Definition
of Self Process

Since that time, which is far enough now, I have often thought that few people know what secrecy there is in the young under terror. No matter how unreasonable the terror, so that it be terror. (Dickens, 1861/2009, p. 30)

Having built a full time outpatient psychotherapy practice by 1992, but becoming more and more dissatisfied with the therapeutic tools I had at hand, I began the development of the hypnosis based trauma therapy protocol I have since named the *Re-Definition of Self Process (RDS Process)*. I came up with this name because clients come to define themselves differently over time with the use of the protocol, changing underlying limited definitions of who they have been.

It became a core resource in my practice, evolving over time as I paid attention to what was useful to my clients. It is a protocol I have used over many thousands of hours in therapy sessions and have taught in workshops nationally and internationally for twenty-five years. As a private practice clinician with no university affiliation, I have no research published to back up its effectiveness in resolving trauma. I only have my clinical experience and the experiences of other therapists who have included this protocol in their own work.

When writing a paper about the protocol in the late 90's, I struggled to find a way to represent what I understood to be happening when I did this work. As someone trained in systems theories I recognized the importance of feedback loops as they applied to families and how the changes in one individual in the group would affect the entire group. It occurred to me that what I was doing with individuals in therapy could also be understood as affecting an internal feedback loop and I came up with the following diagram to represent this as an *Intra-personal system* (Wilson, 1999, p. 152).

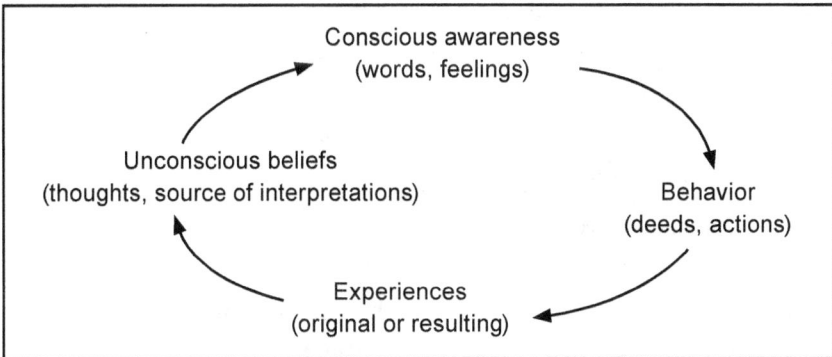

Figure 4.1: Intra-Personal System

I explained it as follows. From before birth,

> An individual has experiences which contribute to the development of unconsciously held defining beliefs about self and self in relation to others, a sense of who they are. These beliefs create who they become in conscious awareness, the words and feelings used to describe self, consciously. Subsequent behavior, as an expression of self, influences experience which is then interpreted by the unconsciously held beliefs to effectively maintain a pre-dictable and, for many individuals, a limited existence. (Wilson, 1999, p.152)

When my daughter was a high school student, she did an art project where she molded wire mesh to the shape of her face and stapled this to a board she had painted with a Yin-Yang design. She then attached a small mirror to the forehead of the mask. When I asked her what the mirror was about, she simply stated, "I am a reflection of my environment." I have used a photograph of this project on the cover of the book. Her life experiences with others outside of herself influenced who she came to know herself to be.

Conceptualizing Figure 4.1 as representing an *Intrapersonal system*, one learns about self in relationship to the world around them and maintains this learning until an external impact at any point in this system disrupts the feedback loop and triggers new learning in the entire system. These disruptions, including therapy interventions that focus on beliefs, feelings, behaviors, and experiences, act as mediators of change and influence the occurrence of markers of change (new beliefs, feelings, behaviors, and experiences) within the individual.

I knew that in the protocol I had developed I was addressing the unconscious beliefs that were the source of interpretation for life experiences. These beliefs were affecting the entire feedback loop of self-identity. Much later, after learning the details of the biological pathway for trauma memory resolution, I recognized how this pathway is embedded in the structure of the protocol I have developed. I now understand why the protocol is as effective as I, and many of my clients, have found it to be.

The Re-Definition of Self Process is a protocol that is based on an understanding of how to use hypnosis to access unconscious awareness. Hypnosis is a tool that is useful in the context of therapy, not therapy on its own. At the same time, many practitioners of clinical hypnosis would not recognize the hypnotic elements present in the protocol. To be used most effectively by a clinician, basic training in Ericksonian hypnosis is a recommended precursor to using the protocol.

In this chapter, I will present the protocol in detail, providing a lot of clinical examples. I will do this in parallel with the sequencing specified in Appendix A. Appendix A offers a practical summary of the detailed description of the protocol and facilitates its adoption into practice by therapists who are already comfortable dealing with trauma issues. Snippets of recorded dialogue from actual therapy sessions, from published transcripts, and paraphrased examples will illustrate the various points in the protocol and some of the variations that can occur in practice. When a client came into my office I would gather some basic information from them, as well as ask what had brought them into therapy. Even in a first therapy session, if I had thirty minutes left to do a piece of work, I would use this protocol with the client. Early positive experiences in therapy will motivate an individual to continue with the work. I have defined four steps in the protocol and will list these along with the parallel elements in the trauma resolution pathway. Even though I have retired from the practice of psychotherapy, I will describe the protocol as if I still use it presently. This will be more effective in facilitating its adaptation by others.

Step One: Responses as Resources – Memory Activation and Retrieval

Daily events trigger emotional and physical responses that may not appear to be contextually appropriate to the moment because these events *activate* a fear-based memory and lead to the re-creation of the emotional and physiological historical context in which the fear learning took place. These responses are a client's presenting complaints, such as anxiety or anger, and they become resources when they are utilized via the following suggestions to facilitate memory *retrieval.*

I have the client describe their emotional response and how they experience it physically. A middle-aged woman recognized that she was always willing to jump into rescuing others, often at her own expense. She described it this way: "I almost can't stand to see someone else suffer. Intellectually I know it's not my problem, but even the thought of it makes me anxious." She felt this anxiety in the pit of her stomach.

Utilizing a hypnotic suggestion as an induction to facilitate an altered state of awareness, I ask the client to externalize and visualize the response. I use a question such as: "If you could see a picture of this response, what would you see?" Most people will easily visualize a response, but others, like myself, do not have that sensory preference. Their individual preference can often be determined by listening to the language they use: visual, kines-thetic, auditory, olfactory or gustatory predicates in their speech. In that case, use a sensory suggestion that they indicate such as: "If you could hear what this response was saying to you, what would the words be?"

What is visualized or heard is the metaphorical represen-tation of the emotional and physiological response that has been triggered. Metaphors are commonly used in everyday speech and are an effective tool to use in referencing experience. For example, feeling betrayed is often expressed as someone stabbing you in the back; an unwelcome surprise may be expressed as having the rug pulled out from under you. Using the response and its metaphorical representation as the focus for inquiry allows the client to become curious and to move further into a trance state, accessing unconscious awareness while bypassing logic, justifi-cation, and fear.

The depth of the trance state that is facilitated is client specific, utilizing innate hypnotizability. Almost all clients work in a mixed state of awareness, maintaining conscious awareness while accessing unconscious material. Depth of trance is not a limiting factor in the use of this process. It can be just as effective for someone who is moderately hypnotizable as it is for someone who is highly hypnotizable.

In the example of the woman who became anxious over the suffering of others, the anxiety in the pit of her stomach was seen as "a cliff." I asked her to immerse herself in this metaphorical visualization. This suggestion assists in the deepening of the trance state, intensifying and narrowing the focus of attention internally for the client. Asking questions such as: "What is it like inside the image?" or, "Is it comfortable or uncomfortable?" will provide further information for both the client and the therapist. Her response was, "it's very scary and doesn't feel safe; feels like I could fall off." Asking someone to put himself or herself into an image of a snake, a fire, a tornado or a volcano, can frighten them. I remind them that it is only an image they are creating, ensuring they maintain some connection with conscious awareness while doing this work.

I believe in the protective and benevolent nature of the unconscious and I assume positive intent, even though that may not be directly apparent in the symptoms and metaphors that clients present. While immersed in the image, I have the client ask for its purpose or what it is doing to or for them. I suggest that the client pay attention to the first thing that comes to mind. For this woman the answer was, "it's a caution, there to scare me, to keep me on the edge." A common response to this question is, "it's trying to protect me." Sometimes the response is, "it's trying to kill me!" Even this can be understood to have a positive intent, as living with the ongoing consequences of trauma may have been difficult to endure, and resignation (giving in to dying), may have been seen as the lesser of two evils. At this point, I simply accept what comes up for the client. If no answer comes to mind this question will be asked again, in a modified form, in the final step of the protocol.

So far, we have activated a memory and now we want to retrieve it. In this case example, we hope to identify where this anxious response has come from. To do this I have the client ask the metaphorical image where, when, or how it originated or, at what age it became part of their experience. The usual response will be retrieval of a memory or the awareness of a particular age, even just as a number. This will usually identify the original learning experience, the event that triggered the development of the response.

The answer for this woman was five or six years old. She described the memory saying she saw her father spank her two younger siblings "very hard" and this was "really scary". When a client responds with a much older age, I will ask if there was anything younger. I am interested in accessing the origin of the response rather than experiences later in life that triggered the same response, such as the experience the client is currently presenting with. The veracity of the memory or age that comes up for a client is not as important as the meaning that client has made of the experience. It is the meaning, for example: "I am at risk," that has resulted in the creation of the problematic response, such as, "I must be vigilant."

In some cases, the recalled memory is directly related to a recent trauma. A young woman who had been severely injured was experiencing PTSD symptoms in the year after her recovery. Recalling the event in my office, she said, "I feel sick, my heart is starting to go faster, my palms are sweating and I'm going to go flying through the air and there is nothing I can do to stop it; everything is out of control!" For her, the accident was the source memory.

If the original experience is very emotionally threatening the client may, when asked about the origin, become numb emotionally or experience psychosomatic symptoms such as a sudden intense headache, nausea, or panic. I recognize these reactions as warning signs from their unconscious telling the client to go no further. Appreciating their self-protective unconscious intentions, I have the client thank their unconscious mind for being cautious. I also have the client ask their unconscious to work with them to help them feel better.

In keeping them grounded to the present, while accessing the past, I remind them that this is a different environment where the purpose is to be helpful, not harmful. The fear they feel in the moment of remembering is the fear they felt at a younger age, and as I usually worked with adults, not how their adult selves would feel in the same circumstance. This deliberate dissociation prevents the abreactions that clients may experience when they feel they are reliving the past.

With this reassurance, the numbness, headache, nausea or panic reaction will cease and the original experience will come to mind. A professional man felt anxious about his upcoming retirement. When asked to access the source of the metaphor for this anxiety, he exhibited a full-blown panic attack. Calming him with words like those above, he then revealed the source of the trauma. "When I was a young child, my uncle was murdered. My uncle was like a father to me because I didn't have a father." This sudden change in the course of his life set him up to have anxiety over proposed changes in his future.

The following exchange demonstrates the previous points regarding recalled age and distress with retrieval of a trauma memory. This woman described the anxiety she felt as being in a whirlwind, seen as the metaphorical image of a child's metal "spinning top".

Therapist: And where is the spinning top coming from? What age, what moment did it come to be part of your life telling you, you were losing control? (Client: Oh shit, I'm like 26.) Anything younger than that? (C: No) Ask it if it's anything younger than 26 (client appears more upset) and remind yourself you are sitting in this office now and you'd like to learn more about where this top has come from, to help yourself feel better. Your distress just now is a warning and it's trying to take care of you. Where, when, or how did this spinning top first come to be part of your life? C: I'm like 6, it's wintertime; my dad is drunk, he's fallen in the bushes; my mum says we have to leave him there. (T: And...) It makes me sad, like I have to save him.

(When no original experience is identifiable, I find the response that has been triggered is more of a habit that has outlived its usefulness than a response still tied to any unresolved trauma. I would then go to the questioning and resolution of the need for the metaphorical representation and the reactive response, as described in step four.)

The final suggestion in this first step of the protocol is to ask the client to speak to the past self that they have identified. I have them specifically ask the past self what they would like *from* the current self (not for but from) in order to feel *more okay*. The phrasing of the question implies the existence of some resourceful abilities in the past. An additional question here that will usually elicit an answer is: "What is he/she afraid of?" For the client in the first example, she responded by saying that the child self wanted "safety for herself and for her siblings because she's always scared they're going to die." For most clients, responses express a desire for reassurances that are missing in the midst of crisis.

Step Two: Experiential Learning – Memory Labilization and Updating

So far, we have completed the activation and retrieval in the pathway toward fear memory resolution. In this step of the protocol I am offering clients the opportunity to experience themselves differently in relation to the trauma memory they have recalled. I am attempting to assist the client in bridging the gap in time from the original learning experience to the present moment, to update awareness. In order to do so, the fear-based memory needs to first become *labilized* or destabilized. The safe therapeutic setting and the first three questions/suggestions in this step facilitate awareness that there has been a mismatch between expectations and current experience.

Once labilized, the original memory is *updated via the remaining questions and suggestions that are experientially meaningful to the client in relation to the trauma memory.* I have the client imagine talking to their past self in the retrieved memory, in order to facilitate the re-working of the meaning of the past experience and to resolve the emotional content and impact of that experience.

The client will ask the past self what it was like for them in that moment. This is a request for a description, not for a reliving of the moment as an abreaction. This questioning usually facilitates an empathic understanding and compassionate connection with the past self. The past self may not recognize the current self as trustworthy. The client I am working with may be seen as just another adult, a stranger who may be dangerous. If there is hesitation to share experiences from the past, have the past self "check out" the current self to determine a level of safety. Use a suggestion such as, "show that past self the kind of person you are." Elaborate this request with details the client has told you about themselves as a parent, sibling, or friend to others. With safety established, continue with the questions and suggestions.

For the woman who witnessed the spanking of her siblings, she described her child self, "getting hit every day; she's scared all the time. But it's even scarier when her sisters and brothers get hit. She's always trying to please. She wonders why she's being hit. She wonders why all these bad things happen."

The next question is to ask what the past self imagined their future would be. The longitudinal research of Lenore Terr, studying the traumatic effects of a children's school bus hijacking in Chowchilla, California, in 1976, identified a common thread. Victims of childhood trauma stop imagining that they will have a future (1990). Most of the responses to this question are therefore distressing: fear of a continuation of the trauma they are experiencing; fear of abandonment; or, a fear of dying. All of these responses express a sense of powerlessness and imply dire predictions about the future.

In order to further labilize or destabilize the fear memory, as well as introduce the first piece of relevant new information that will update the fear memory, this next suggestion is crucial.

I ask the client to imagine bringing the past self forward in time to sit next to the current self, showing that past self their future, who they've become today. This exercise reinforces the necessary mismatch of expectations; not only have the conditioned stimuli been terminated with no reinforcement of the unconditioned stimuli, but also *the fear memory's predictions about the future have not been realized.*

There can be resistance to accepting that the current self is their future self. To overcome this, I employ suggestions such as: "Show them an imagined video of your life and the common elements of family" or, "Show them that you remember the events of the memory." At times though, there may be a lot of animosity towards the self in the past experience; harsh judgment and condemnation that reflect an individual's self hate.

Another client, a University student, came in with a "fear of self-sabotage" as she had recently been skipping classes and not doing assignments. She localized the fear in her stomach and saw it as a dark shadow where she could hide to keep herself safe. This metaphorical image came from age fifteen when she had dropped out of school and left home as a rebellious teenager. This client described her fifteen year old self as someone "I have been hating and fighting for a long time." When I asked her if that fifteen-year-old self had deliberately done what she did with the intention of screwing up her own future, the client responded with "no." That teenager had just wanted to get away from the circumstances she was in.

What may be seen in hindsight as a regrettable life choice may come to be understood in a more positive light as this communication with the past self is facilitated. Another client resented her younger self for getting sick, an illness that led to multiple abdominal surgeries and scarring over time. That younger self did not choose or like the illness either! As well, there can be judgment expressed by the past self towards the future self for not living up to early expectations. It is important to clear these obstacles to connection with the present, as in the example of the woman who saw her father in the bushes.

> Therapist: Bring the little girl forward in time and sit her beside you now and show her the woman she is today. (Client shakes her head no.) What's that about? C: I feel desperate. She's shaking her ... (finger shaking at herself).)
> T: I want her to see who she is today, that she actually grew up to be an adult person who has more choices in her life than she had at age 6; that she didn't die. Show her the efforts you've made to become the best person you can be. It's not okay for this little girl to be shaking her finger at you. The anxiety you're feeling now is hers. You're a lot further ahead in life than she was at age six. C: The more you talk, I feel like she's taking the weights off.

With resolution of these conflicts, it is common for the past self to experience surprise, liking, and appreciation for whom they've become. As well, this experience begins the process of updating the fear memory. Some of the powerlessness has been eliminated as a result of the awareness that they have moved past the trauma.

The next series of questions and suggestions do more to update the fear memory. They are no different than what may be used in the process of cognitive restructuring except that, in this circumstance, they are applied directly to unconsciously held beliefs – implicit memory that has been brought to conscious awareness. They serve to challenge these long held beliefs and eliminate the limitations they have created for the individual.

If the past self did not get what they thought they needed to manage their own survival, or were harmed in some devastating way, how did they become the person they are today? This question has the client recognize the fact that, as proven by their ongoing existence, that they were capable of finding ways to take care of themselves. This brings to conscious awareness innate resourcefulness that has been active and unaltered over time. Some approaches to therapy suggest that the current self should take care of and protect the past vulnerable selves that emerge. I find this to be insulting. The current self only exists because of the strengths of the original self that have sustained them. As this middle aged man with addiction and anxiety issues declared in this example:

> Therapist: Does he see that he was never as vulnerable as he thought he was? Client: Yeah, actually. And that's been proven with, again, like looking at me now and through time, that I'm stronger than I ever thought at given points. I always thought, well, this is it; this is the end, now I'm going to just collapse and completely disintegrate as a human being. And it never happened. ... He has a lot more inside than he ever thought (Wilson, 2005, p. 75).

What motivated the individual to keep going? If life experiences are horrendous, it is understandable that someone might give up on living. From early on, individuals experience interactions with the world around them and come to know themselves via feedback from that world. If the feedback is repeatedly unloving in nature, it is very common for those individuals to conclude that they are unlovable. Being small, dependent beings, means they need others to provide for their necessities of life. To conclude that there is something inadequate or wrong with the caregivers who are not meeting their needs would result in a sense of hopelessness. They cannot "fix" the caregiver and don't have the option of going elsewhere. On the other hand, if they believe they are the problem, maybe they can do something to fix themselves, to earn the caring they need. This illusion of empowerment engenders hope for survival. It's the only option to latch on to in order to keep going.

Even with the establishment of an unconscious belief and identity of not being loveable or being a worthy human being, there is some underlying hope that this isn't true. This hope drives people to seek out therapy. Simultaneously, they harbor a fear that this is true. I have had the experience of clients (often children of unwanted pregnancies) being very afraid to look too closely at this belief. Not knowing for sure, one way or the other, still allows for hope, whereas looking too closely might reveal the worst of their fears and abolish all hope. At the same time, not looking may prevent the individual from knowing the best outcome: a shift in identity to being a loveable, worthy human being. When these clients have taken the chance of courageously examining that belief, I've watched them discover the best outcome for themselves every time. Personally, I have no doubt in that being the only outcome they will experience. Every newborn is worthy of being cherished, just because they exist.

There must always be an element of hope for the future in order to keep moving forward. In helping the client change the core belief of being unlovable, an essential question to ask is: "Does anyone make an effort for anything they don't care about?" Clients have exhibited a determination to stay alive. They have life accomplishments. At the very least, they are in a therapist's office facing their own demons in an attempt to be healthier. All of this is evidence of their caring about and loving themselves. These efforts have previously never been consciously recognized or overtly expressed as self-love. Understanding that this loving of self is proof that they were loveable (because I have loved me, I am loveable) eliminates the belief of unworthiness, created in the past in relationships with others, and establishes the new belief of being loveable as self determined.

It is never enough for a therapist to care about a client. Unless clients see themselves as worthy of caring, no caring from others will be accepted for what it is. Therefore, the relationship with the therapist is not the most important relationship for clients engaged in psychotherapy. *The most important relationship is the new one they establish with themselves,* and knowing themselves as loveable and valuable is a fundamental shift in their self-awareness.

I have often found that clients will take on responsibility for what is not theirs to own while not being responsible for what is. Reversing this is essential to regaining health. Having the client ask the past self if they were responsible for the events that happened to them begins this correction. They will often claim they were responsible, because they were told that their behavior, or even existence, made the other person do what they did. Children want to make sense of their experiences and will latch on to anything that explains what has been happening to them. My client, who was hit a lot, said of her child self, "she feels bad a lot of the time, like she's bad or wrong. If she makes noise, if she doesn't do well at school, if her room is messy, if everything isn't perfect – then bad things happen."

Many experiences of abuse are easily identified as both emotionally and physically painful. There is congruency in this assessment. This congruency may be lacking when it comes to experiences of sexual abuse where induced sexual arousal may be physically pleasurable while the circumstances are abhorrent. Abusers capitalize on this confusion in order to shift the blame onto their victims. Clearing this confusion is critical to releasing responsibility for the sexual abuse. I will ask clients if their eyes choose what they see, or if their ears choose what they hear. Our senses don't choose their perceptions; they just respond to stimulation as they are biologically designed to do. Their bodies are not to blame for what has been done to them.

Clearing the false beliefs of responsibility opens up the possibility of the client being able to see the past self as innocent. The past selves must also come to know their own innocence. For this client, dealing with a trauma memory of sexual abuse, this was crucial.

Therapist: And who is this little girl who's in pain? … Is she someone who deserves that abuse? Client: No, but she thinks she does. Somehow she thinks she deserved it. T: Ask her to show you; what is there so wrong with her that she deserved that? C: There is nothing wrong with her. T: Ok, but she doesn't necessarily know that herself. So ask her what she thinks is wrong with her, to show it to you so you can help her decide. Can she prove to you that she deserved to be abused the way she was? ... C: (Voice affect calmer and assertive) When I ask her that question she can't find anything. Nothing comes up. T: Who is she showing you that she is? ... C: She's innocent, she's trusting (Wilson, 1999, p.156-157).

If claims of responsibility continue to be expressed, I will ask the client how they made other people do what they did. How did they get inside the other person's head and determine their response for them? I propose the opposite as well, suggesting that if they could make them behave in harmful ways they must have had the power to make them behave in caring ways too. I question what the response behavior of others says about whom those others chose to be. This line of questioning challenges the assumed responsibility and authority over the behavioral choices of others. I will often say: "Sorry, you were not that powerful. No one is able to decide for another person how that other person is going to act."

These questions also challenge the evaluation of the client's behavior, needs, or even existence, as problematic. One young woman, who judged herself harshly, learned that her child self wanted to be loved. She recognized that "nobody cared enough" and felt that things would have been better if she'd been "different somehow, just a different kid." As a preschooler who was left alone and lonely, she was "always doing stupid things." She saw her child self as a "rotten person," and concluded that she was rotten because, "it just has to be, because I can't think of anything else, just all the events, always upsetting people." This client's contempt for herself was easier to accept than recognizing the neglectful behavior of her parents.

Children, in the position of being dependent on others for their survival, have little choice over where to place the blame. If they were to see their parents as being at fault, they would feel helpless to manage their own survival. Some do try, such as a three year old who made her way to her aunt's house to tell her aunt she wanted to live with her, or a four year old who packed what he thought were essential supplies and went off down the road to fend for himself. These events were oft repeated as amusing family anecdotes! For the majority, blaming themselves offers some hope of redemption. If they can figure out how to do things right or be different, they hope it will make their life better.

To help dispel this illusion that they could have got what they wanted from the people important to them, I ask the client to show the past self the consistency of the bad behavior of those others over time. Very often clients feel they were singled out for mistreatment. It is useful to have them recognize how even a favored sibling has not been loved any more than they were because that favoritism had to be earned. The appearance of caring was a conditional trading process for both siblings. No one who knows that love is a gift of caring, with no strings attached, can love one child and not love another.

I also ask the client if they have known those people who had hurt them to have ever behaved in the way they would have liked them to behave. These questions help the client to recognize that the hurtful behavior of others was an expression of who those others chose to be and had nothing to do with the client and who they were. Those others were going to do what they did regardless of who was in front of them.

Occasionally clients have been reluctant to give up the special status they had when they did earn attention from a parent for being, for example, "such a big helper." Recognizing how they had been taken advantage of in taking care of the adult, vs. being cared for by the adult, may be hard to accept. Traditional expressions, such as "children should be seen and not heard" exemplify this warped sense of who is responsible for whom. People who were praised for being so "mature" when they were young, were often left to take care of themselves, victims of neglect painted in a positive light. A child not having needs made life easier for the parent.

Clients have often told me in defense of their parents that they "did their best." I counter with the words that the parents did what they knew how to do; they did not pay attention to the impact of what they did in order to improve upon it. Children, in their nature and in their dependent position, will love their parents unreservedly. Many a client has had difficulty finding fault with their parents because this has felt like a betrayal of their love for the parents. I remind them that if you honor someone, you do not lie about them. I help them to understand that loving their flawed parents comes from them as an expression of who they are and that it is possible to love someone whose behavior you do not like and will not tolerate. The two feelings are not mutually exclusive. This helps relieve guilt over being honest about their feelings towards their harmful or neglectful caregivers.

Often a client experiences regret for choices they have made as a result of the old beliefs. Via an imagined review by the client, the past self may be shown the consequences of those erroneous beliefs and offered the opportunity to apologize to the current self. This apology is usually not needed by the current self but is useful to the past self. Old beliefs that have caused distress over time, such as despondency that manifests as depression, or guilt that has resulted in self-recrimination, or any belief that has had negative consequences for the client, may be apologized for. The current self will then accept the apology.

The apology allows the client to make peace with themselves. They put down a long carried burden. The word "relief" is the most common response to the question of: "How does the past self feel when you, (the current self), accept their apology?" As well, clients have often known punishments to be out of proportion to any crime they committed and they may

be averse to admitting responsibility. An experience of accountability that is emotionally freeing, as opposed to humiliating, is
novel. Without fear of reprisals, it becomes safer for the client to
admit to mistakes. This opens up the possibility of taking more
appropriate responsibility for themselves in future.

The woman who saw her father in the bushes had a
disturbing image, of a "fetus in a sac, curled and shrinking,"
appear during the course of this work. She had spent many years
feeling severely anxious and depressed. Of the image, her six
year old past self said: "This could be me." The client continued,
saying,

> I feel like she wished for a long time that that was what
> happened instead of coming all the way here. Does that
> make sense? T: That she wished she had just disappeared?
> C: That she had just shriveled away and disappeared
> instead of coming all the way through and been born. I
> feel like she forever wished that she just didn't make it all
> the way. T: Because it was so hard? (C: Yes) And is that
> understandable? (C: Yes) And if she knew back then her
> own resourcefulness, her own strength, her own ability
> to deal with things, would she have ever been so caught
> up in that desperation? (C: No) And did that weigh on
> you a lot over time? (C: Yes) So would she say to you: "I'm
> sorry I ever underestimated my own resources." (C: Yes)
> And do you accept her apology? (C: I do) And how does
> she feel? C: Good, she wants to walk on the clouds. T: So
> she's feeling lighter? C: Relieved.

I expect that everyone could say: "If I knew then what I
know now, I would have done things differently." It is a truism
that can be expressed and accepted as an apology. Some clients
will still harbor resentment and anger towards a past self for
those misguided life choices and this needs to be cleared before
an apology can be accepted. In that case I ask the client to consciously and directly tell them off. They have already been

attacking themselves unconsciously for most of their lives. This suggestion makes the option of attack overt. In the context of this work, and the empathy they have developed in coming to know themselves differently, they will usually find they are unable to do this. They can no longer maintain the animosity towards the past self. The anger and resentment vanish and the apology is accepted.

The final question in this step of the process is to determine if there is anything more that the past self would like to tell the current self about the past experience. It is important to resolve any remaining emotional content, especially feelings of anger or sadness. As long as a child is afraid, that child is not safe to express anger. With the fear eliminated, the current self can silently witness and validate the internal expression of these emotions. A comment from the therapist, such as, "there is nothing a child could ever be, do, or say, to justify how you were treated" is a reinforcing validation. I have often said that if we all had validation of our experiences from day one, we would have no need for therapy later in life.

Step two is the most time consuming part of the protocol and occasionally takes more than one session to complete. If a second session is needed for this piece of work to be completed, the memory retrieval is direct and it is not necessary to repeat step one for this specific memory. It is expected that there has already been some updating of the memory and once this updating and emotional resolution of the past experience has been completed, the therapist can then proceed to the next step. As well, I have found that in working with clients with Dissociative Identity Disorder (DID), resolving the trauma memories to this point was as far as we would go in each session. Only when enough emotional resolution had occurred, over many sessions with many issues, were we then able to proceed.

Step Three: Fusion of Experiences – Memory Updating

The third step involves bringing the past and present together to create congruency, a cognitive restructuring that includes both conscious and unconscious awareness. For clients with DID, this also means fusion of personalities. More *updating* of the fear-based memory is facilitated with additional questions and suggestions.

In this step, I ask the client to focus again on the past self sitting next to them. I want to know how they feel sitting side-by-side. Fusion is not possible with any animosity, fear, or distrust between them. These feelings need to be cleared, as exemplified in the following exchange I had with the aforementioned client dealing with her sexual abuse history.

> Client: She's a little tentative, a little apprehensive, scared to trust. Therapist: Do you accept that? C: Yes … T: And how is that for her as you accept that about her? C: Lets her guard down a bit, now she's not, not holding back as much (Wilson, 1999, p. 157).

A common fear is of having to take care of the past self, burdening the client's already burdened life. In the example of the rebellious fifteen year old past self, the client said, "I can't carry her because she's too heavy. She can be a burden." When I asked if that past self wanted to be carried, the response was "no, in fact she resents that." And the reverse can be true. The same client said the fifteen-year-old past self "thinks she needs to take care of me" because that teenager had been expected to take care of her parents. As well, the client said the teenager self was "worried she's just going to mess me up more." Her response was to laugh and say to the past self she couldn't do more than she'd already done.

Another fear is that the vulnerability of the past self will be more dominant in their lives. The client feels the vulnerability of the past self in their lives currently because of the separateness. With fusion, the past self will no longer be alone and stuck in the past experience and the vulnerability will be diminished.

Once mutual comfort has been established between the present self and the past self, I confirm the presence of resources in the past self that will enrich the client's current self. What does the past self know now, about himself or herself, that they did not know before? Through the process of updating, clients will often have recognized resources of strength, persistence, intelligence, and so on. What I emphasize at this point is the specific identification of resilience, innocence, lovability, and value.

Resilience, the ability to bounce back from adversity, is evidenced by their existence now. Clients can readily own this resource as they reflect on all that they have overcome.

Innocence is often the hardest resource for the client to accept. What was done to them was shameful; they were innocent victims who did not ask to be harmed. Regrettable behavior in reaction to what was done to them does not mean that they were born malicious. I firmly believe that children are born innocent and completely vulnerable in their dependency. They offer their caregivers an opportunity to rise above themselves to become the best they can be. Unfortunately, many people do not take this gift. Instead, they pass on the harm they experienced in their own lives. (I'll go into this more in the next chapter.)

Clients recognize that they are loveable and valuable because they have loved and valued themselves. Their efforts, to hang onto the best in themselves and to keep moving forward in time in spite of the adversity, show them that they have worked for what they cared about. Once these resources have been identified I will say something similar to this:

> Feel the two of you sliding together now, like a double image focusing into one. As you come together, sharing who you are with each other, the past self gets to know in the experience of who they are today, their own *success*.

No matter how vulnerable they were, the past self was able to figure out what they needed to do to keep moving forward in time, to hang onto themselves, to become the person you are now. And if you could figure out what you needed to do from that younger age, you are going to figure out what you need to do from now on with all the resources you have to work with now. (This last sentence is also a post-hypnotic suggestion for future progress. It's a prediction based on experience and is readily accepted by the client.)

The only security we can ever have is when we feel in control of our lives. The only control we can ever have is in how we choose to respond to life experiences. Everything else is outside of us. For the client, recognizing that they have been able to successfully respond to life experiences over time, there is an enhancement of their personal security and self-efficacy. They come to trust in themselves to deal with what comes their way.

I emphasize the word success. That is not usually a word that clients use to describe themselves and this is a significant reframing of their life experiences up to this point. By sharing who they are with each other, consciously reclaiming innate resourcefulness and owning progressive life skills, the client and their past self integrate the past experiences within their current reality. The person they are now is living proof of their success. This is the most convincing evidence that needs no outside verification. They know it to be true because it is their lived experience.

For clients with DID, the idea of fusion triggers fears of loss. I remind these clients that their ability to dissociate is not something I can take away from them. As well, I cannot force their personalities to stay together. I suggest they test out fusion and then separate again, to prove to themselves that they have that choice and to tell me how it felt to share whom they are with each other. With the clients that I have worked with, all have retained that association. The total is always greater than the sum of the parts.

Step Four: Checking – Updated Consolidation

Once we have completed the first three steps in the protocol, it is important to find out if it has made any difference for the client. It does not matter what I think of myself as a therapist, what matters is whether or not clients experience something useful! With the following questions and suggestions I check for evidence of change: changes in the emotional content and meaning of the trauma memory; changes in self-identification; changes in the metaphorical representation of their symptoms; and, changes in their reactivity. All of these changes demonstrate the initial phase of *updated consolidation*, evidence that the new information has become incorporated into the previous memory structure.

After fusion, I ask how the client feels. I expect comments such as, "it feels comforting," or, "it feels right," or " I feel more complete." If I don't hear and observe these expressions, fusion may not have occurred. I go back to check for obstacles of fear or distrust. Do not accept the current self "taking care of" the past self. The focus is a mutually respectful sharing of resources. The client, who saw her father in the bushes and had experienced the use of this protocol during previous sessions, described the fusion this way:

> It's good. It weirds me out that every time you say that, I feel like I vacuum her up. That's how I feel. It's not a yucky feeling, its just, it's weird because I can physically see somebody and they just kinda go "shuup" (making a suctioning noise and motion).

When I am certain that fusion has occurred, I want to check on the fear memory. I have the client recall the past experience. It should be less meaningful, distant, or neutral in affect. For the client just mentioned, I asked her to:

T: Think back to being that six year old standing there being told to leave him lying in the bushes. How does that moment feel now? (C: Deserving) What does that mean? C: Like she feels he deserves to be in that bush. Like, ugh, how could you be so stupid? You deserve to be there, you put yourself there. She just kinda looks out the door and shakes her head and walks away. T: So she's not taking any responsibility for that? (C: No) And would she leave him lying there indefinitely? C: She knows he wakes up and comes home by himself (expressed with a sly grin on her face!).

The woman who was dealing with childhood sexual abuse described the experience of fusion, and the trauma memory image as follows:

I went through a, sort of a tiredness, … wanting to sleep, … but it's from the, from having a, maybe a place of refuge, a place to, to be accepted and realize she's not alone. T: And how's that feel now, with her a part of you, the two of you together? C: It feels like she never left. T: Ok, now I want you to remember that image, the one you saw earlier in the month and the one you saw today of that little girl curled up on the floor. How does that image feel now? C: I just scoop her up and, and together we say, ok, now let's get on with the rest of the world, with the rest of our life! Now it doesn't have, it's not stopping me, it's not got a lot of emotion tied to it" (Wilson, 1999, p. 157).

The client who needed to save others from suffering said the original memory now "feels sad, it doesn't feel terrifying. It feels more like a memory instead of happening in the moment." The middle-aged man with anxiety and addiction issues, expressed his review of the trauma memory with these words:

It doesn't feel as chaotic, it doesn't feel as out of control because there's a, it's like I picture this little boy and he's

got like, suddenly, has this anchor, an internal anchor. …
It doesn't matter where you are, perhaps … I guess what
matters is what you are, what you've got inside (Wilson,
2005, p. 76).

If there is any remaining sadness or anger about the past
experience, simple validation is usually all that is needed to
let it go. The unconscious mind holds the emotional content of
experience in a timeless way. With resolution of the emotional
content of experience, the past events become part of the client's
history. The old emotional reactivity is no longer expressed as
part of their current lives.

Next, I check on the metaphorical representation of the
presenting complaint. It will often be recalled as having changed.
As a variation on the question asked in step one that more directly
declares a positive intent, I ask how it has tried to be useful to the
client. Trusting in unconsciously motivated self-care, I believe that
the metaphor has been created as a survival or coping strategy.
Referencing the client examples previously described: the "cliff"
image kept that client vigilantly cautious; the metal spinning top,
the kind that you would pump with a handle, told her she was
losing control and that she needed to act to regain some control of
her life; the dark shadow kept that client safe as "nobody bothers
me in there".

If the client has not previously identified this usefulness,
I will offer options for a positive perception. A client who
suppressed her anger described how she got "this feeling like
a tight rock in my chest and my jaw gets really stressed; like I
want to clamp my jaw shut, basically." She saw this response as
"a big boulder." She felt frustrated and angry immersed in the
image and described the boulder as wanting her "to be motivated
to do something." The positive intent was not obvious until she
understood that containing her anger in that boulder was a pre-
requisite to being loved.

As a child, protesting about an undesirable task was not allowed. Shaming meant being a "bad girl" and was accompanied by emotional withdrawal. Keeping her "jaw shut" stifled her feelings and gave her the opportunity to behave better and earn the approval she needed. Understandably, this strategy never resolved the underlying issue of not feeling innately worthy of love. It created a double bind for her: if she protested she was bad and if she didn't protest she was still bad because she was angry inside. That identity of badness made her feel unlovable.

I then ask if the client needs this metaphorical representation any longer. Many reply saying that they don't want it, but that is very different from any perceived need. This learned response to the stresses they've had in their lives has been a tool they have used over many years and they are often reluctant to give it up! For others there is greater ease in letting it go.

For example, with the cliff image, the client responded by saying, "yes it was useful and I don't want it to keep me on edge at all." I repeated the question asking if she needed it to make her cautious, to which she replied "No." The client who visualized the spinning top didn't need it to warn her that she was out of control. Things were more complicated when it came to the dark shadow. When I asked if she needed that hiding place, the client responded by saying, "I need it to hide my abilities and now I don't know why I need to do that." I then asked her to take the dark shadow inside herself, to see if it fit any longer. She responded with "not really, no, it's like going in the wrong way and it's not comfortable." Asking her if it had served her to hide her abilities, she responded by saying,

It was the only way I got attention, by doing bad things and ignoring my abilities that everyone was so proud of. Oh my god, I just realized that I'd perform well for a while for recognition and then be taken for granted, so I would stop doing it. Being good didn't get me what I wanted.

Checking to see if the metaphorical response fits anymore, by asking the client to take it back inside themselves, is a useful challenge to help them identify this response as no longer being necessary in their lives.

Not needing this response does not mean it goes away. Some therapeutic approaches suggest various means of disposing of these strategies. I find it much more effective for the client to be genuinely appreciative of their own unconsciously generated responses that were created to assist them. Asking the client to embrace the metaphorical representation while thanking it will often bring on that emotion of gratitude. Reassuring the meta-phorical representation that the individual has shown the ability to take care of themselves over time, allows the metaphorical representation to vanish. This letting go can be a complicated process! Here is some of the dialogue in two such cases. For the spinning top metaphor,

> T: Do you need this top to be worrying about you, saying: "be careful, grab on to things, try to hold them still"? (C: No) So thank it for the job it did when it was thought to be necessary for you to have a sense of control over your life. (Client smiles) And what's happening. C: It's starting to rust. Slow, like "eee, eee", (acting out the motion) when you push it. I feel like it's time for it to go. It got rusty and went, it's like this (indicating a tiny size between her thumb and index finger). It's like, it has to stop spinning, (making a spinning motion with her fingers). T: Pick it up and gently hold it in your hand. Say thank you very much for worrying about you, "I'm more okay than you thought I was." (Moves her hand close to her face and gently blows at her hand.) And what's happened? C: It's gone now. I blowed it away. T: You blew it away? (C: Yes) I don't want you blowing it away. (C: Why?) It's not your job to blow it away. (C: Ah, I want to.) I know you do. I want you to very gently hold it, thank it and reassure

it saying: "It's okay dear, I know you've been worrying about me and actually, the one control nobody can take away from me is who I choose to be and I've hung on to myself all these years in spite of the world around me and I will continue to do that." And what happens to it as you genuinely reassure and appreciate it? C: (With melancholy) It melts away.

In previous sessions, as she thanked the metaphorical image for what it had done for her, she would then have a furrowed brow. When I asked her what that was about, she said: "When I thank it, as it goes away it waves goodbye."

For the client with the dark shadow, it was an equally difficult farewell. She wanted to keep it nearby to hide her abilities so "I will always need someone to take care of me." She had a long held belief that dependency assured her of loving attention. I asked her if this strategy had worked for her. She responded saying that it hadn't, and instead had made her feel worse about herself. It kept her safe but stuck. With thanking the shadow, it vanished. She concluded by saying: "It feels odd, because with it gone I see open space. Life is open to me now. But I now know that I don't need to be scared to be on my own because I'm a very capable person!"

With resolution of this metaphorical representation of the presenting emotional issue, I then go back to the beginning, asking the client to revisit the issue they brought to the therapy session. I ask them to pay attention to any emotional or physical reactivity to the issue, as they review it in their minds. The presenting response will have changed or disappeared altogether. The client who was so worried about the suffering of others was a care giving professional. When she thought about how she would feel now over the suffering of others, she said:

I don't want to be taking on other people's issues. I had been noticing that I'd get anxious, worrying about how to take care of others when they really could act to take care of themselves. That's not good for them. I would take their ability to cope away. When I think of them now, I feel calm. My stomach knot is gone.

The University student who was worried about self-sabotage said, "it's my choice. I don't feel like it's going to get me. I have control and it's not controlling me. I'm surprised that I am capable of taking control of my life. It's nice. I feel good and I don't hate that fifteen year old me and I've been hating her for a long time."

The middle-aged man with anxiety and addiction issues, unfamiliar with being comfortable and afraid that things were too good to last, said:

It doesn't feel quite the same now; it doesn't feel as frightening. For starters, there is nothing saying that things are going to fall apart, but I feel like if changes happen for whatever circumstance, it doesn't mean that I have to crumble as a person. T: And you also had a fear that you will somehow set it up for yourself, sabotage yourself. How do you feel now about that fear? C: Well, I feel kind of a quiet assurance that I don't have to; I don't have to do that. And maybe through the years I've always felt that I had to in order to feel comfortable again. T: And so how does your chest feel now? C: I don't feel that same tightness or anxiety (Wilson, 2005, p. 77).

I also ask the client to imagine a future situation, similar to the one they presented with, and to be curious as to how they see themselves responding. Because of the fundamental changes to their unconscious beliefs about self and self in the world, clients will describe a new awareness, and imagine new behavioral actions and outcomes.

Any residual response often signals the need for more work to be done, using the same approach with this residual response. This next piece of work usually brings up a different learning experience, or fear-based memory. Once a piece of work has been completed, the triggering event no longer results in the emotional and physical reactivation of the context of the fear-based memory because that fear-based memory no longer exists in its original form. It has been permanently changed with the new protein formation altering its biological structure, the process occurring during updated reconsolidation of the memory trace (Nader, Schafe & LeDoux, 2000). It is very common for clients to feel physically tired after doing this work. Sleep allows for the reinforcement of the new learning in the second phase of the updated reconsolidation.

Prior to ending the session, clients are instructed to be observant of their own behavior between therapy sessions and to pay close attention to how they find themselves responding. In the next therapy session, I ask what they have noticed. Because the changes are generated spontaneously at an unconscious level, clients may be consciously unaware of how they have responded differently. They will tell me that the week has been uneventful, but on further questioning, we will identify moments that previously would have caused distress for them. Instead, they now find themselves at ease. Therefore, it is important to check with them for evidence of change in their daily lives.

One client, who had a history of being bullied as a young child, would make an effort to please others in order to be safe and to be cared about. He would usually neglect his own well being in doing this, prioritizing family and friends, and feeling resentful in the process. Once this issue was resolved, he described his new experiences during the week following that therapy session. His mother had called asking about a cooking issue. He responded to her saying,

"You need to figure these things out on your own since you've been cooking longer than me" and then we actually laughed about it. I didn't have that tense feeling and I didn't get frustrated and yell and get all worked up, which is usually what would happen.

He also found that he was able to say yes to a request by his employer, no longer fearing that his doing so might upset his peers.

Further comments he made during this follow-up session relate to the impact this work can have on marital relationships. His wife noticed a change in his behavior, recognizing that he was more willing to assert himself. He reported her saying, "before, what you'd do, you'd get angry and kind of force the issue, but now you're like 'no, I'd rather not do that right now'." She had noticed that he didn't get frustrated by a lot of things. He would previously react to her stress and during that week,

> It was almost a lack of reacting to her stress, because when she gets stressed I will try and do anything that I could possibly do to take her stress away. When she gets stressed about her work, there is nothing I can do except to do the normal things around the house that helps her out. Instead of automatically thinking there is something I can do, I have to do it to make her happy, or to help her solve her problem, or to get her unstressed, there is nothing I can do because it's not mine to solve. For her, she needed to get it done and she was stressed about it. But I couldn't help her with it. It was something she had to do on her own and I was more able to let that go.

I met with his wife soon after and, not surprisingly, the issue she brought up related to how he had changed. When her husband had said no to her request to do a chore for her, he had wanted to finish doing the dishes first! When he did not immediately jump in to appease her, she had responded with silent withdrawal, what she referred to as her "blank mode." This included a desire to retaliate, holding a grudge emotionally against him. He asked her why she was angry and, for the first time, she saw her response as an expression of anger. She also saw that it was out of proportion to the situation and was her issue, not his. She recognized how she internalized her anger while forcing herself to do what she did not want to do. I described her experience earlier in reference to the "big boulder" that represented her feeling like she had to clamp her jaw shut. Resolving this internal conflict with herself helped her more readily accept herself, allowing her to openly express her dislike of having to do an undesirable chore while still being a loveable person.

As a result of working with individuals and recognizing the impact that change in one member of a couple had on their partner, in 1999 I expanded on the diagram representing the internal workings of one person to describe the dynamic in a dyad. I refer to this as an *Inter-personal system* where the changes in one member of the dyad impact and may facilitate changes in the other. All relationships are dyads as we interact with everyone else uniquely. This diagram as Figure 4.2 looks like this.

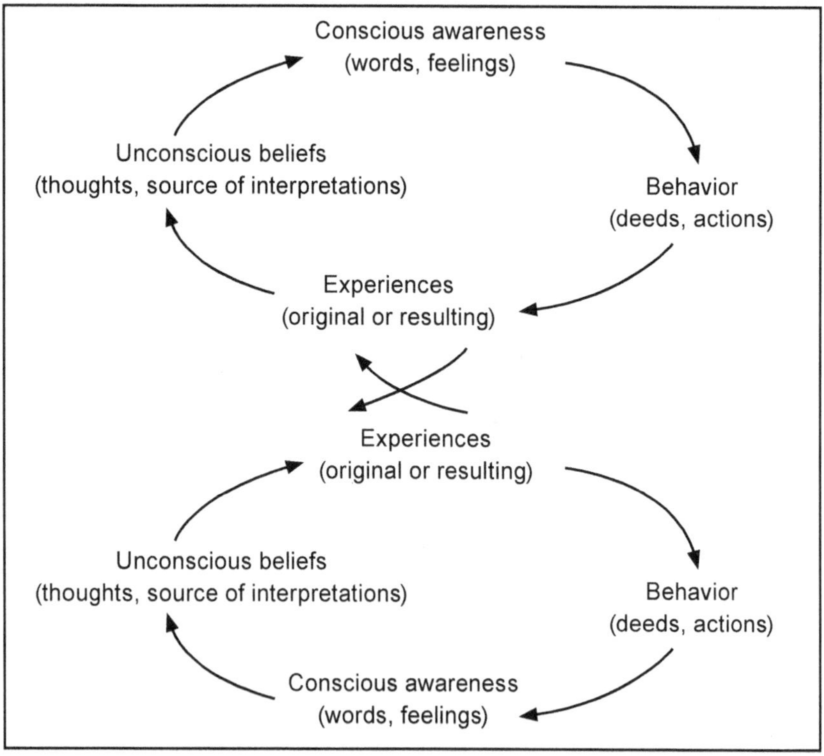

Figure 4.2: Inter-personal System

I have watched this dynamic in action with couples that were willing to own their own reactivity in their relationship, especially when their spouse no longer gave them an easy out. When the husband in the previous example stopped rescuing his wife, and did not get upset himself, the issue fell back on her. Fortunately she was willing to deal with it. I refer to this back-and-forth effect as people who "leap frog" off each other's growth. Schnarch talks about "marriage's intricate people-growing machine: it invites you to stretch yourself and your re-lationship" (1998, p. 153). The Inter-Personal System figure may represent this machine in action. All meaningful relationships are challenged to grow this way.

When I worked with couples, I saw them individually initially. If they were seeking therapy, they probably didn't trust their partner with their own vulnerability, especially in relation to early childhood trauma. Resolving one's personal issues, while the partner resolves their own, eliminates the mutually triggering events that cause conflict between them. Eventually, the partners felt safe to do their own work in the presence of and with the support of their partner, an experience for both that deepened their emotional intimacy.

Unfortunately, both members of a couple may not be willing to address their own contributions to relationship struggles. Schnarch refers to the dynamic of being pumped up by the emotional fusion of a reactive spouse as "borrowed func-tioning" (1998, p. 66). One member of a couple may only appear emotionally healthy when their spouse isn't doing so well and they don't like it when the tables are turned. As the non-reactive spouse no longer takes on the issues their partner will not own, the borrowed functioning diminishes. The partner may then leave the relationship.

In terms of personal growth, the move is lateral as opposed to vertical. The spouse who has outgrown the dysfunctional dynamic may also give up on attempts to bring their partner along with them and may end the relationship. They will move on with greater ease and choose healthier relationships in future. We all act as mirrors to each other. When we do not like what is reflected back to us, we can either dismiss it, examine it, absorb what is useful, or just smash the mirror. With divorce rates as high as they are, there are a lot of mirrors being smashed out there.

With some clients, it is not possible to proceed through the four steps of the protocol as described. A very rare occurrence is when someone is extremely hypnotizable. Such an individual could go into a somnambulistic trance where they do not readily communicate verbally. When this has happened, I have adapted the protocol to use questions with a yes or no response option so that idiomotoric signaling (as simple as a nod for yes and a sideways shake of the head for no) can be used to communicate. With children, it is possible to have the child draw an image of their face in the trauma memory and have them address the questions to the image. Responses can be spoken or written, depending on their comfort level. A smiling image, drawn at the end of the session, will demonstrate resolution of the emotional content of the memory. The important element in these variations is the inclusion of the suggestions and questions that allow for updating of the labilized trauma memory.

As well, clients will often present in a session with concerns over disturbing dreams. I have them recount the dream to me, but rather than attempting to interpret the meaning of the dream, I have them focus on their emotional and physiological response to it. I then use this protocol to resolve the dream turmoil. From my point of view, these dreams represent the surfacing of unconsciously held material from unresolved trauma.

Clients will often report that they felt good for the first few days after doing this work, but in the day or two prior to their next therapy session something else surfaces to nag them emotionally. People will often think they have regressed when this happens. Apparent setbacks are just the emergence of new work, commonly surfacing as recurring thoughts, dreams, or new reactivity, and these new aspects of awareness are addressed in subsequent therapy sessions. I understand this as their own unconscious mind generating a line up, with a new issue saying "me next." Instead of regressing, I watch these individuals progressively empty the "storage cupboard" of their unresolved emotional issues while they stockpile their resources.

With all the new learning, the reclaiming of innate resourcefulness, and the establishment of self-trust, clients expand their repertoire of life skills. Because the new learning is at an unconscious level as well as a conscious one, clients often recognize the impact of the work after they have found themselves behaving differently. They surprise themselves with their own spontaneity. The learning is retained. Clients rewrite the meaning of their histories. The past events remain the same but the perceived impact on the present and future is changed. They move from merely coping, to thriving in life.

I recognize that most of the examples used in this chapter reference traumas from early childhood. We do establish a worldview, and how we fit into it, very early in life as a necessity of evolutionary survival. How we become primed to respond to life experiences is the topic of the next chapter and will explain why so many of the issues individuals deal with as adults stem from early life learning. Past experiences, that have never been emotionally resolved, remain current and affect our lives indefinitely. Effective trauma therapy makes them part of our history and frees us to move forward, unshackled by the past. Finally, as promised in the conclusion of the last chapter, I have identified the effective utilization of the pathway for fear-based memory transformation in the four-step structure of my protocol.

References

Dickens, C. (1861/2009). *Great Expectations* (150 Anniversary Ed.) New York: Penguin.

Nader, K., Schafe, G. E., & LeDoux, J. E. (2000). Fear memories require protein synthesis in the amygdala for reconsolidation after retrieval. *Nature, 406*, 722-726.

Schnarch, D. (1998). *Passionate marriage: Keeping love & intimacy alive in committed relationships*. New York: Owl Books.

Terr, L. (1990). *Too scared to cry: How trauma affects children and ultimately us all*. New York: Basic Books.

Wilson, M. A. (1999). Responses as resources in the integration of experience. *Hypnos, 26*, p. 151-158.

Wilson, M. A. (2005). Comparing the hypnotically based re-definition of self process to EMDR. *Hypnos, 32*, p. 67-81.

CHAPTER FOUR

Secure Attachment, Efficacy and Resilience

I am writing this book during the pandemic of COVID-19. I wonder how much posttraumatic stress will surface following the immense losses experienced worldwide. This moment in time has me thinking about the pandemic of the Spanish Flu a century ago, one that our ancestors survived. I am a fan of the well known BBC series Downton Abbey, (2010-2015). In that series, the family of the main characters experience many losses associated with that time in our medical and world history, a young woman dying shortly after childbirth, another young woman dying of the Spanish Flu and a young man dying in a car accident on the day of his son's birth.

One might think that this much tragedy occurring in one family is unrealistic. Except that it isn't. My own family experienced more. My paternal grandfather was born in 1883, married in 1907 and had a son in 1908, an uncle I knew. From the stories passed down in the family and what I can source in ancestry records, he had another son born in 1909 who died in 1911. In 1913, his wife and their third child, a daughter aged three, died of influenza. He married again in 1915 and had a daughter in 1916, an aunt I knew as well. His second wife and her unborn child died, during childbirth, in 1918. He married a third time and my father was born in 1922, the first of six more children.

During the dirty 30's my grandfather survived being gored by a bull and my father quit school to take over running the farm. In 1955, my dad's next brother, the fourth living child, was killed in a car accident, his wife left an institutionalized, bedridden quadriplegic and their six month old baby then raised by the mother's family. My grandfather lived to the age of eighty-five, dying when I was an adolescent. You might think that the family tragedies ended there, but no. A year after my grandfather's death, the son and daughter-in-law of his oldest son were killed as the result of a propane explosion on my uncle's farm, leaving their orphaned baby to be raised by extended family. At least that was one tragedy that my grandfather did not have to live through.

It would not be surprising if, after so many tragic losses, my grandfather had become an embittered, despondent man. He never spoke English and I have few memories of him, but what I do remember is a very gentle, and quietly loving man. As well, my father was one of the most generous and loving people I've ever known. The question is: how did my grandfather maintain the best of who he was, and pass that on to the next generation, in the face of so much trauma and tragedy in his own life? Where did his resilience come from?

The research into Attachment has some of the answers. Siegel, in his book *The Developing Mind* (1999), provides a simple definition of this concept. "Attachment at its core is based on parental sensitivity and responsivity to the child's signals, which allow for collaborative parent-child communication. Contingent communication gives rise to secure attachment. . . . Suboptimal attachments arise with repeated patterns of non-contingent communication" (p. 117).

Mary Ainsworth was the researcher primarily responsible for observing and describing what secure and insecure attachment looks like. An aspect of this research not usually referred to is how she began these observations in the first month of an infant's life, doing four-hour-long home visits with families for a total of eighteen visits over 54 weeks. What is striking is that she was able to observe "characteristic mother-infant interaction patterns during the first three months" (Bretherton, 1992, p. 765) that related to the infant behavior observed in a laboratory setting when the babies were one year of age.

The development and the employment of her Strange Situation laboratory procedure (Ainsworth, Blehar, Waters & Wall, 1978), where one-year-old babies were stressed by separation from their mothers (the primary caregivers at that time), followed this extended period of at home observation. Ainsworth found herself becoming more interested by the "patterns of infant reunion behavior" (Bretherton, p. 765) than in the general behavior displayed in the presence of the parent. These reunion behavior patterns were attachment strategies "for eliciting protection and comfort from their busy parents" (Crittenden, 2017, p. 438).

These patterns were initially classified into one category of secure attachment and two categories of insecure attachment, (Ainsworth et al., 1978), with a third distinct category of insecurity identified at a later date (Main & Solomom, 1986). These categories are: Secure; Avoidant; Resistant or Ambivalent; and, Disorganized/Disoriented.

While Ainsworth was conducting her research, Bowlby, a long time collaborator of hers, was writing his trilogy of books on the topic of attachment: Attachment (1969), Separation (1973), and Loss (1980). He had realized that "he had to develop a new theory of motivation and behavior control . . . [and that] . . . the ultimate functions of behavioral systems controlling attachment, parenting, mating, feeding and exploration are survival and pro-creation" (Bretherton, 1992, p. 766). Any organism that did this had to "have evolved an ability to construct internal working models of the environment and of their own actions in it" (Bretherton, p. 766) in order to predict the behavior of the attachment figure and to plan for their own response. As well, he

recognized that the internal working models became self-reinforcing over time. This reflects the concept I described earlier in
reference to the *Intra-personal system* diagram from chapter four
reprinted here (Wilson, 1999, p. 152).

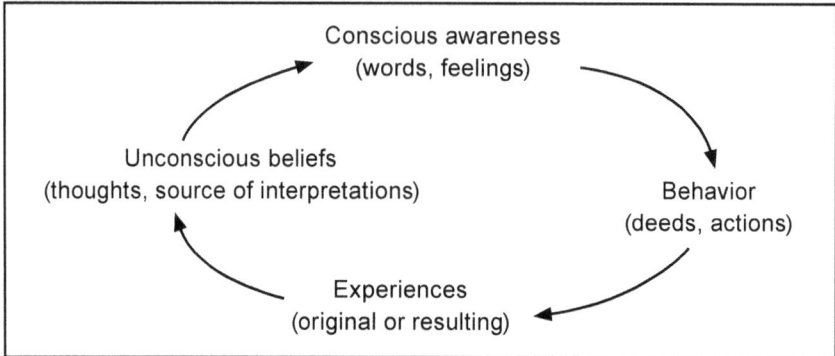

Figure 5.1: Intra-Personal System

This diagram may be seen as an internal working model
of attachment as it meets all the criteria of the new theory that
Bowlby found was needed. It visually represents how experien-
tial learning results in decisions regarding behavior and motiva-
tional control, is self-reinforcing, and allows for predictions about
future interactions. I'll refer to the previous example I described
concerning my daughter at age three when she responded to her
grandmother telling her she could stop crying because "it didn't
hurt anymore." I will assume that my daughter's internal working
model, that defined her level of emotional security, was that her
own perceptions were to be trusted and that her experience of
pain justified her tears.

In spite of her grandmother being a figure of authority, her
self-awareness supported and predicted how she would respond
to having her feelings dismissed by another. She held on to
herself and reinforced that self-trust. At the same time, someone
who does not trust their own perceptions will accept the invalidation of others. The invalidation will then reinforce the lack of
self-trust.

Bowlby also elucidated "the role of internal working
models in the interpersonal transmission of attachment patterns"

(Bretherton, p. 767), a concept that clearly expressed the importance of nurture in child rearing practices. The second diagram of an *Inter-personal system* may represent what occurs with the transmission of attachment patterns from one generation to the next. For example, a parent with a strong sense of self-awareness will validate and reinforce the self-awareness of a child. The reverse is also true. The internal working model of what life experience means and prescribes for feelings, behavior and expectations will be set and reinforced by the attachment figure.

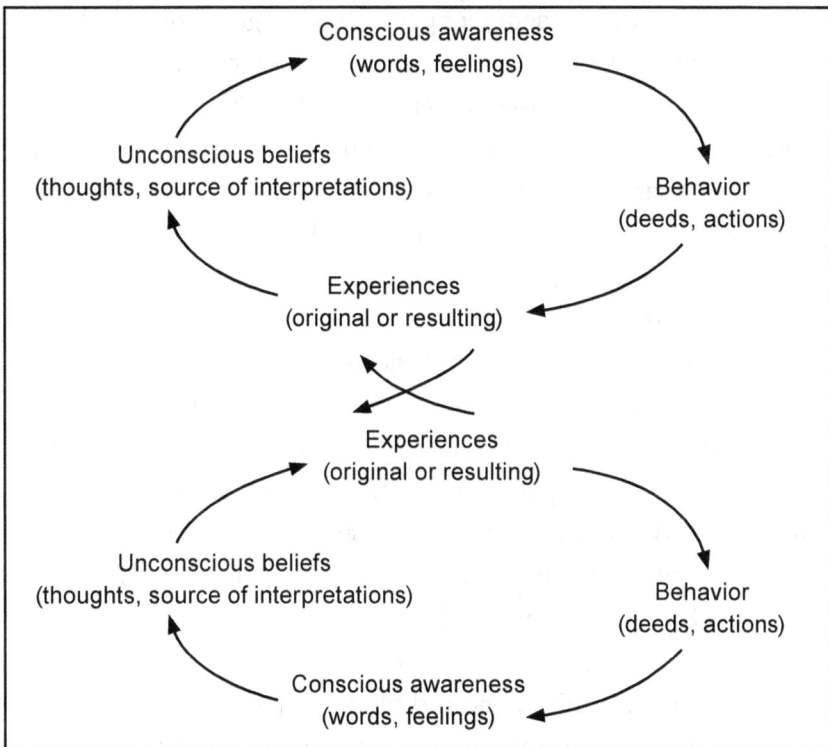

Figure 5.2: Inter-personal System

During the last ten years of his life, Bowlby became focused on the application of Attachment Theory to the practice of psychotherapy, with therapists attempting to become the secure base for clients as they reworked their internal model of attachment (Bretherton, p. 768). In attending trauma therapy conferences, I have observed that this approach appears to have become a dominant strategy as therapists assume the role of caring, reparative attachment figures. I find this to be an approach that has limited effectiveness for reasons I have expressed previously. Caring in the present moment does not change the experience of not being cared about in the past.

Progressing from the work of Bowlby and Ainsworth, there was interest in learning more about the internal working models of attachment in the parents of the children they studied. To this end, the Adult Attachment Interview (AAI), a structured series of open-ended questions, was developed to identify categories of adult attachment patterns (George, Kaplan, & Main, 1985). Initially, one category of secure attachment was identified along with two of insecure attachment. A third category of insecure attachment was discovered later (Main & Solomon, 1986) and these four categories directly correlated with the four categories for childhood attachment. These were identified as: Secure/Autonomous; Dismissing; Preoccupied; and Unresolved/ Disorganized.

In early 1981, following the birth of my first child, my mother was visiting. She was conscious of the fact that I was very responsive to my baby's needs. After she left, she sent me a small clipping from a newspaper article she had read on the flight home. It quoted Dr. Minde, a neonatologist working with premature babies in the neonatal intensive care unit of the Sick Children's Hospital in Toronto, Canada. He said: "Even a baby two days old is an organizer of his environment. He already knows how to get things done for him" (Globe and Mail, February, 1981).

I assume that my mother was indirectly and scornfully telling me that I was at the beck and call of my daughter. Many years later when I repeated the quote to a colleague, her immediate response was to say that the baby was "spoiled". At two days of age? Mary Ainsworth had to deal with challenges claiming that maternal responsiveness would spoil a child. She countered by saying, "an infant whose mother's responsiveness helps him to achieve his ends develops confidence in his own ability to control what happens to him" (Bell & Ainsworth, 1972, p. 1188). This statement sums up what I believe is the fundamental importance of an internal working model of attachment: control gained through observations and conclusions that offer predictions about future interactions.

Human babies are born completely dependent on others for their survival needs, but they are not passive participants in their own existence. They have a very limited repertoire of behaviors by which to make their needs known to their caregivers. The results of their efforts will help them build or lose confidence in their communication strategies. Confidence requires a trust in one's ability to be effective in any pursuit, to figure things out, and confers a sense of security. For the infant, the pursuit is survival.

Repeated failures to elicit appropriate responses in their communication with caregivers will begin to erode an infant's belief in their efficacy. The failures tell them that they are not capable of having control over their lives. This results in insecurity.

I will describe the behavioral patterns exhibited in the various categories of infant and adult attachment style and what these behaviors tell us about that child's sense of efficacy. The behavioral descriptions are gleaned from the chapter titled Attachment in Siegel's book, (1999, p. 67-120), as well as personal experience. The comments concerning evidence of efficacy, or its absence, are my own.

Secure/Autonomous Adult - Secure Child

A Secure/Autonomous parent behaves as if they are attuned to their child, able to read the infant's signals and respond appropriately. They know when to pay attention and to calmly do something for the infant, and when to disengage, allowing the child personal space. They also know how to repair disruptions in communication, to re-establish coherence. A Secure infant in the laboratory study will explore the space while the parent is present and then show signs of missing the parent when the parent leaves, including crying. After being left alone for three minutes, on the parent's return the infant will go to the parent, make physical contact, and stay physically close until settled. They will then return to playing.

What the behavior of the infant tells me is that the child has the confidence to ask for what they need and to expect that comfort and reassurance in return, trusting that their communication strategies will be effective. Repeated successful experiences in dyadic communication with the caregiver have reinforced this sense of efficacy; "I can trust myself to be effective in the pursuit of my own survival; I have figured out what I need to do to give me some control over my life."

My daughter displayed this efficacy as a teenager. In conversation with me, she was attempting to decide on her educational direction after high school. She finally said: "Oh well, I've lived a charmed life up until now, I'm sure I'll figure it out." I was surprised by her declaration; I did not think her life had been charmed. She'd had to deal with experiences that would challenge any child, but she'd had help in resolving those difficult moments as they happened and they had not undermined her security. More than twenty years later she continues to live up to her prediction of figuring things out.

Dismissing Adult – Avoidant Child

In the first category of Insecure Attachment, the Dismissing Adult is someone who will meet the basic survival needs of their infant, but will be dismissive or even blind to the emotional needs of the baby. They are more likely to leave the baby to cry itself to sleep, dismissing cries as meaningless. They may also be neglectful and rejecting towards the infant. Their Avoidant categorized infants will display indifference to the presence or absence of the parent in the Strange Situation lab studies. They will explore and play independently, will not show any emotion with the absence or return of the parent, and will not seek contact.

The infants of these parents have learned that their repeated attempts to communicate their needs have failed. So they stop trying. Their apparent emotional indifference is belied by the fact that their heart rates will change and their cortisol levels will go up, both indicators of physiological stress (Spangler & Grossman, 1993, p. 1439). By one year of age they are already demonstrating a disconnect between their emotional expression and their physical experience. Their behavior is saying: "I have not been effective in my communication strategies and I have given up expecting to be heard or understood by this person. I am resigned to doing life on my own but I don't trust myself to be able to figure out what I need to do. I'm not certain I can manage my own needs." I recall two male clients who displayed the effects of being raised in this way, both having difficulty maintaining an emotional connection with their wives. One man had spent the first part of his life in an orphanage; the other man was the child I mentioned previously who had packed his bag and left home at age four.

Preoccupied Adult – Resistant /Ambivalent Child

In the next category of Insecure Attachment, the Preoccupied parent will be caught up in the drama of their own life. They project their own turmoil onto their children with un-predicable and abrupt shifts in mood. They will appear oblivious to the emotional or physical needs of the child, and then will suddenly focus on the child, imposing their own needs for attention or affection. There is an incongruency in communica-tion, signals get crossed as these parents do not appear to have the ability to be attuned to the infant.

In the lab research, the Resistant/Ambivalent infants of such parents display a wariness or distress even before being separated from the parent. They are preoccupied in their focus on the parent, appearing to try to figure out what will come next. They will cry inconsolably when the parent returns and will not settle. Their behavior seems to be saying: "I'm trying to read the signals from this person, but I can't figure out what is going on or predict what will happen next. My attempts to communicate do not result in a consistent response. I don't know if I can handle this uncertainty, this lack of control over my survival." One mother I've known, whose husband died accidentally while she was pregnant, was intensely bereaved for the remainder of the pregnancy and after the birth. It was part of the family lore that the infant cried incessantly for the first year of his life. Clients, who have displayed this emotionally unpredictable behavior, had family histories of parents with similar attributes. They, in turn, displayed very little awareness of the impact of their behavior on the well being of their children.

Unresolved/Disorganized Adult - Disorganized/ Disoriented Child

The final category of Insecure Attachment in an adult is Unresolved/Disorganized attachment. These parents often have serious, unresolved trauma histories and they may consciously or unconsciously re-enact the traumas of their own lives with their children. These parents may behave in fear-inducing or confusing ways that overtly scare the infant.

Their Disorganized/Disoriented infants display behavior that is dramatically different from infants in the previous categories. The behavior is nonsensical, with or without the presence of the parent. At a conference a few years ago, a researcher using the Strange Situation protocol in his work, demonstrated the behavior of one of these infants on the return of the parent to the room. Moving sideways, he shuffled to his right across the stage, while leaning to his left. The distressed infants in these family contexts want comfort from the parent while simultaneously knowing the parent to be the source of their fear. Being caught in a paradoxical bind, these infants have been observed to move toward a parent, then to abruptly veer away before collapsing in a trance like state. They appear to be saying: "I want to believe that I can get my needs met by this person, but my experience tells me that I will be harmed instead; I've got nowhere to go and nothing to do to help myself. I give up, I am powerless to get my needs met."

Having worked with many clients who were harmed by the people they depended on, I know too well the enormity of the emotional conflicts created in such dynamics. They display complex and severe symptomatology that requires significant psychological repair in order to establish emotional security.

Beyond these four paired categories of Attachment, Siegel also describes "an informal subset of secure/autonomous adults [who have] an 'earned', secure/autonomous status" (1999, p. 91). These are individuals who, according to the descriptive events in their personal narratives, appear to have been raised by parents that were insecurely attached and, as a result, they should display those same insecurities. This subset of adults doesn't do that. There may have been attachments that were established with others, that were unique to each of those relationships, which mitigated some of the damage done in the more unhealthy attachments. Regardless of the source, either via relationships with others and/or through efforts of their own, these individuals have resolved the insecurity they would have experienced with their insecurely attached parents.

> If this 'earned' category truly represents the emotional development of an individual from an insecure to a secure/autonomous state of mind with respect to attachment, then the narrative coherence within the AAI may reflect some important integrative process that enables parents to break the transgenerational passage of insecure attachment patterns (Siegel, 1999, p. 92).

Of great significance is this observation: *the behavior of the infants of this subset (of 'earned' attachment parents) is indistinguishable from the infants of securely attached parents (Siegel, p. 92)*. This is a message that I have passed on to my clients who have earned their emotional security through the work of trauma therapy. They have fears that their children will have the same problems as they have had and this awareness, of a potentially healthy outcome for their children, is very reassuring for them.

This research into understanding how people become emotionally secure or insecure has been applied in the area of prevention. Changes in how children are cared for in orphanages and parental presence for children who are hospitalized are two examples of where this research has influenced childcare. This research also provides a foundational understanding of the origins of the symptomatology clients present with in therapy.

Another definition for insecurity is a state where one is "beset by fear and anxiety" (Merriam-Webster's Collegiate Dictionary, 1993). Almost all psychological symptoms are based in fear. Siegel's discussion of attachment theory research supports this notion. A meta-analysis of Adult Attachment Interviews "indicates that insecure attachment appears to be associated with a higher incidence of psychiatric disturbance, including anxiety and mood disorders" (Siegel, 1999, p. 86) and "in psychiatric populations, insecurity in the AAI is far more prevalent and security . . . is far less prevalent than in the general population" (Siegel, 1999, p. 87). Insecure people live in a state of chronic fear that varies in intensity and is expressed as their symptomatology. Their insecurity, in not knowing their own efficacy, leaves them handicapped to deal with what life brings their way.

How Attachment research is applied to the practice of therapy is the next issue. If individuals can earn a state of secure attachment, and raise securely attached children as a result, future generationally transmitted insecurities will be eliminated. How do we facilitate this earned attachment for our clients? *Is our work as therapists one of providing a reparative attachment figure (our relationship with them) for our clients, or one of facilitating the identification of efficacy in our clients (their relationship with themselves)?* As I've described in chapter four, the focus of my work has been changing the relationship clients have with themselves.

I offer another example here to reinforce this approach. In 1997 I attended a trauma therapy workshop presented by the psychiatrists, Drs. Herbert and David Spiegel. David Spiegel described his experience with one of his inpatients. The patient, while taking a break from working on highway construction, was sitting atop a barrel set up as a barrier to traffic. A car came through the barrier and hit him, breaking his leg. He recovered from his physical injuries but did not recover emotionally; he sank into a depression requiring ongoing hospitalization.

While hypnotized, this man recalled that in the moment before impact he had *pulled himself back*, an action that saved his life. With this conscious identification of his personal efficacy, he made a full emotional recovery. As Dr. Spiegel told this story, I recalled the experiences of a child I knew personally. That six-year-old boy had entered the parking lot of his ski school, gliding on his skis. Unable to stop himself in time, he had been backed over by his ski instructor who was reversing in a half-ton truck. The boy had his leg broken. Soon after the accident, he told his parents that he had *pulled himself back* so that the truck tire rolled over his legs instead of his belly.

His recovery was uneventful and he continued to ski, including racing competitively as an adolescent. I asked Dr. Spiegel why this child was able to immediately consciously know and express his own efficacy, in saving himself from more serious injury, when his patient had only been able to recognize this with the use of hypnosis. He did not have an answer for me at the time. Only later did I come to recognize that this child had always been conscious of, and allowed to own, his own efficacy. His parents had raised him to be securely attached.

From this, and my professional experience as a trauma therapist, I have come to realize that emotional security is the substance of the protective resiliency that allows some people to continue to thrive while others crumble in the face of adversity. People who are emotionally secure trust themselves to be able to figure things out and move forward when responding to life events. Helping clients rediscover their own efficacy provides them with that resiliency.

I am now able to answer the question of how my grandfather did what he did. He was emotionally secure and that security resulted in his being resilient. He trusted himself to figure things out, each step of the way, and to keep moving forward in time. Like the punching toy clown, no matter how many times it was hit, it would always stand upright again. He lived that reality; he always got up again.

References

Ainsworth, M. D. S., Blehar, M. C., Waters, E., & Wall, S. (1978). *Patterns of attachment: A psychological study of the Strange Situation*. Hillsdale, JJ: Erlbaum.

Bell, S., M., & Ainsworth, M. D. S. (1972). Infant crying and maternal responsiveness. *Child Development, 43*, 1171-1190.

Bowlby, J. (1969). *Attachment and loss, Vol.1: Attachment*. New York: Basic Books.

Bowlby, J. (1973). *Attachment and loss, Vol. 2: Separation*. New York: Basic Books.

Bowlby, J. (1980a). *Attachment and loss, Vol. 3: Loss*. New York: Basic Books.

Bretherton, I. (1992). The origins of attachment theory: John Bowlby and Mary Ainsworth. *Developmental Psychology, 28(5)*, 759-775.

Crittenden, P. M. (2017). Gifts from Mary Ainsworth and John Bowlby. *Clinical Child Psychology and Psychiatry, 22(3)*, 436-442.

George, C., Kaplan, N., & Main, M. (1985). *The Adult Attachment Interview*. Unpublished manuscript, University of California at Berkeley.

Globe and Mail (February, 1981). Exact date, title, page and author unknown.

Main, M., & Solomon, J. (1986). Discovery of an insecure-disorganized/disoriented attachment pattern: Procedures , findings and implications for the classification of behavior. In T. B. Brazelton & M. W. Yogman (Eds.), *Affective development in infancy*, (pp. 95–124). Norwood NJ: Ablex.

Merriam-Webster's collegiate dictionary (10th ed.). (1993). Springfield, MA: Merriam-Webster.

Siegel, D, J. (1999). *The Developing Mind: Toward a neurobiology of interpersonal experience.* New York: The Guilford Press.

Spangler, G., & Grossmann, K. E. (1993). Biobehavioral organization in securely and insecurely attached infants. *Child Development, 64(5),* 1439–1450. https://doi.org/10.2307/1131544

Wilson, M. A. (1999). Responses as resources in the integration of experience. *Hypnos, 26,* p. 151-158.

CHAPTER FIVE

Grief Work

In any therapy work, it is important to acknowledge the underlying grief in the symptomatology presented. Grief is an important emotion that is often overlooked. Effective grieving requires a process of acceptance, a simple acknowledgment of what is, that allows us to say goodbye to what we don't want to say goodbye to. Acceptance has no emotional valence; it does not imply a liking or disliking of any circumstance. It is a grounding in the moment, a still point from which to choose a new direction.

If we lose something that we do not value, we will not grieve that loss. It is only when the loss is important to us, from something as minor as a favorite scarf to the intense pain felt with the death of a family member, that we experience grief. People are generally uncomfortable being around others who are grieving and want to distance themselves from this emotion. I am dismayed with how often people are told they are depressed and prescribed antidepressant medication when what they are doing is appropriately grieving.

To identify this process as pathological is to shame people rather than to honor them. People also self diagnose. I remember a male client who had recently ended his marriage. He came in telling me that he was depressed over this and I immediately reframed his experience as grieving. He was content to have ended an unhealthy relationship but, in the process of doing that, he was also saying goodbye to the future he'd hoped to have. That was a legitimate loss.

Friends, family, acquaintances, and co-workers tell us time will heal and hope it won't take too long! The very limited amount of time allowed as bereavement leave speaks volumes to society's need for others to not feel bad. As a result, grief gets buried and can simmer under the surface for decades.

Even when grief is acknowledged in our western society, we have few strategies that are societally recognized to honor the grief of another. Some traditional religious and ethnic practices are the exception. One of these is the celebration of the Day of the Dead in Mexico where local celebrations allow for beautiful and healing moments for those who are bereaved. When a loved one dies it is painful to think of that person. We may try to distract ourselves from doing so. When we avoid thinking of them, we have truly lost them. Only with effective grieving are we able to have them back in our memories and reminiscences with others. The Indigenous Mexican celebrations of the Day of the Dead allow for that.

Loss, imposed by forces outside of ourselves, occurs with a surrender of the control we hope to have over our own lives. We don't like to surrender control and will resist the apparent unfairness of its occurrence. A child, who does not want to go to sleep at the end of a fun day, does not want the day to end. Simple acknowledgment of it being hard to say goodbye to the day will allow for the letting go to occur.

The day my father turned eighty, he had a vascular incident that impaired his vision. He was forced to stop driving. A few days later, my sister called to ask me to speak to him. He had been short tempered with her and my mother. When I spoke to him he said that he knew he would "just have to get on with things." I told him that it was also legitimate for him to not like the fact that a freedom he'd had from age fifteen was taken away from him. He agreed and his good humor returned. He recovered from the injury and resumed driving a few months later but at age eighty-one, when he was told he'd have to do some updated driver training, he decided to quit driving. He had no grief at that time because he was the one who chose to stop.

A significant amount of disappointment and loss occurs in the conflicts people experience in relationships. With the assumption that we need something from another person in order to take care of ourselves, we put ourselves at their mercy. They have the power to please or disappoint us. The authority over our own well-being rests outside of us and this causes stress. Stress occurs when there is a disconnect between responsibility and authority; we have the responsibility to take care of ourselves but give others the authority over making that happen. This is often the theme of dramas, expressed in lines such as "I can't live without you!"

Whenever there is a discrepancy between what we feel we need in a relationship and what we get from the other person, conflict occurs. If we approach someone with whom we experience some conflict and they hear us out empathically, validating our concerns, the conflict vanishes. The conflicts that persist and cause us distress are those where the other will not do this. As we have no control over who others choose to be or what they have to offer, we may feel powerless. In the practice of psychotherapy clients frequently describe these discrepancies, be it with people from their past or in current relationships.

Back in 1989, I read Sheldon Kopp's book, *If You Meet the Buddha on the Road, Kill Him: The Pilgrimage of Psychotherapy Patients*, (1972). A passage in that book (p. 46-52) described the work he did with one of his clients, a woman who had long standing grievances in her relationship with her mother. Every attempt she made to resolve the issues with her mother had been futile. He suggested that she detail these grievances in a letter to her mother that was not to be sent. She was then to write two reply letters from her mother, one using the words she expected and had often heard before, and the second reply letter being a fantasy expressing the sentiments she had always wanted to hear.

She brought these completed letters to her next therapy session and he had her read the letters to him. This was a powerful exercise that allowed her to express the intensity of her feelings, without restriction, and to give herself the validation she had long desired. She had finally removed herself from the dependency of needing something from her mother, something that would never be offered, in order to feel good herself.

I adopted this exercise into my own therapy practice. Initially, I would verbally describe the task and assign it as homework between sessions. When one woman returned telling me she'd forgotten the instructions, I wrote them out for her. At the next session, she told me she'd lost the paper instructions. I then had her complete the letters during that session. Like Kopp, I had clients read the letters to me. The spoken reading brings on a more profound level of emotional release than does the writing on its own. This client had been afraid of the feelings this writing might unleash. Instead, she resolved her turmoil.

Over time, I augmented the instructions, changed the order of the letters, and typed up a handout that I would send home with my clients. I have taught the use of these letters in workshops and provided attendees with the handout to use in their own practices. A copy of the handout is included as appendix B. At this point, I will go into more detail regarding the context of grieving, the struggles in writing each of these letters, their individual purpose, and various applications.

The title of the handout is: *Grief Work Letter Writing Exercise*. Active grieving is an unwelcome chore and chores only get done when we push ourselves to do them. Avoiding the work doesn't make it go away. As such, I prescribed this letter writing exercise as homework. People are often afraid to begin the process of grieving, afraid they may fall into a bottomless pit of painful emotions. To give them some sense of control, I had clients schedule appointments with themselves to compartmentalize their periods of grief, appointments that had a beginning and an end time. I had them address wayward thoughts that intruded at other times of their day by saying, "thank you, I have an appointment with you later." Doing this, clients did not have to deny their feelings, and like children when acknowledged, their feelings would wait their turn. This letter writing was a useful activity during grief homework appointments. Eventually, clients found that they had no more work to do as they completed the task of grieving.

The handout begins with the following introduction and instructions for the first letter.

Grieving is a process of acceptance and by completing these three letters, you will be able to independently grieve, to come to an acceptance of what is and to let go of what is not. You will be able to say goodbye to what you do not want to say goodbye to. These letters are for your benefit and are not given to anyone, therefore be as open and honest as possible when writing them.

The first letter is written to a person (dead or alive), a past self, or a benevolent higher power, and candidly expresses feelings, wants, likes, dislikes, and disillusionment felt in relation to the experience being written about. This letter must be written with all the intensity that you feel about the subject, in order for it to be useful to you.

The importance of the candidness of expression cannot be overestimated. Long after we had completed her course of therapy sessions, a client called to say that the letters were not working for her. Following a telephone conflict with her ex-husband, she had used this letter writing exercise to try to help herself feel better. As she read out the first letter in my office, I knew what the problem was. The intensity of her feelings, expressed in describing the conflict to me, was not expressed in the writing she had done. Instead, the letter was written in the very polite and courteous way she would have spoken to anyone over the phone. I had her write a more emotionally congruent set of letters during that session and, after reading them aloud, she asked me to shred them to destroy any "incriminating evidence" expressed in the words she had written. She laughed as the session ended, free of the conflict that had distressed her.

Many of our unresolved conflicts may be tied to someone who is no longer alive. A teenage girl was sent to me by her father to deal with such a conflict. When she was a preschooler her mother had committed suicide, leaving the daughter alone and at risk of dying as well. Her father had saved her. I suggested that she could write to her mother about what had occurred and she responded that she couldn't because her mother was dead! Sent home with the task, she finally wrote the letters the night before her next appointment. During her therapy session, I was impressed with the effectiveness of the letters she had written. Earlier that same day, she had finally felt like she was part of the family created by her father and stepmother.

My instructions for the first reply letter are as follows:

Imagining the one written to has received the letter, write a second letter, a fantasy reply letter expressing your most desired response. Include in this letter words that validate your feelings and express accountability. Do not include any justifications, excuses, patronization, or use of the word "but". It may also include an apology of three parts: I'm sorry; it will never happen again; and, what can I do to make it up to you? This fantasy reply letter may be written as a simple "nice" apology or may be written as a courageously honest response, such as: "You are right. I never did like you!" Again, it must validate the feelings of the person, you, doing the three letters.

Kopp was not as specific in his instructions for the three letters as I became. The example from his book of a desired letter includes a lot of justifications (1972, p. 51-52). Justifications and excuses diminish the effectiveness of an apology. Use of the word "but" disqualifies any statement that came before it. Common expressions such as "I'm sorry, but," are meaningless as apologies. These cannot be included in this letter. An apology only becomes meaningful when it is followed by a commitment to change and an action of reparation. Otherwise, words are cheap. A clear and direct apology may be all that is needed to satisfy the fantasy of what the client would like to hear in response to their complaints.

At other times a brutally honest reply, that validates an underlying and long denied truth, may be more appropriate. I learned this from one of my clients. He was the child of an unwanted teenage pregnancy, resented from day one and blamed for changing the course of his father's life. When the father became ill and was given a brief life expectancy, the son's involvement in his care facilitated his living much longer than was predicted. When a younger and more welcome sibling appeared on the scene, the oldest sibling was dismissed. When asked why, the father said, "I never wanted you." As devastating a response as this might appear to be, it freed him from feeling any need for recognition from or obligation towards his father from then on. Honesty is the highest form of love, and with these words his father was the most loving he had ever been towards him.

This letter is also the one that is the most difficult for clients to compose. It is rare for an individual to be told that they have a right to their perceptions and feelings. Instead, their experiences are often dismissed. They are told they cannot "see it that way" or that they are "overreacting" to an issue. As a result, clients often do not know how to validate themselves. They may come in with two reply letters that are essentially the same, with the fantasy reply being a bit more polite than the reply that would be expected. When this happened in my office, I dictated a desired response for the client to record in writing. I had them take the letter home to use as a template for future letters that expressed what they desired to hear.

The second reply letter is easier to write. Clients will have already heard the expected words spoken to them and need only record these in a written form.

Again, imagining receipt of the first letter, this third letter is another reply letter, differing from the one above in that it expresses the expected response. This letter validates the knowledge and experience you have of whom you are writing to. A second reply letter is not necessary when writing to a benevolent higher power, someone deceased, or a past self, because the desired response is also the expected response.

Both reply letters offer validations to the client, one of their feelings, the other of their knowledge and experience. When writing to someone who had died, I suggested to the client that they imagine that person had the power to now know both sides of every story and to have become both wiser and more compassionate. They no longer existed in their limited human form and would no longer offer the expected response. A benevolent higher power, one we are given permission to complain to with these letters, would not give us magical answers but would offer comfort and support. A past self could also be seen as accountable and would only write an emotionally validating response. Sometimes the response of the past self would be necessary self-defense. Attacked for choices made in the past, it was legitimate for the past self to agree that those choices were bad and to be acknowledged for correcting them. There is a time limit to self-recrimination or the punishments do become worse than the crimes.

The last paragraph of the handout is this:

The two reply letters separate the fantasy, the illusion of the most desired response from the reality, based on experience, of the expected response. By doing these letters, you will be able to come closer to acceptance of what is, as separate from the fantasy of what is desired, saying goodbye to illusions that result in disappointment. Acceptance is a beginning point, a solid ground from which to then move forward.

In explaining this last concept, I offer the analogy of driving into a new city without a road map to guide you. You have a destination in mind, and think you know the route, but find yourself going in circles. Until you stop and determine your exact location you cannot choose where to go next. Acceptance of what is, in all aspects of life, is the stopping point that allows you to choose your future path.

Doing these letters does not necessitate ending the relationships written about. I use another analogy to exemplify this, one of asking for a lump sum of money from someone. If they only have a lesser amount to offer, no matter how many times I ask for or demand the original amount, they don't have it to give. I have a choice to politely accept what is offered, or to remain frustrated. There is no point asking for something that does not exist. Acceptance changes expectations and eliminates future disappointments.

One set of letters may unearth another level of grievance and it is then useful for the client to repeat the exercise. Once I was assured that clients knew how to get the best use out of the letters, it became an exercise they could use independently to deal with whatever conflict they encountered.

These letters may be used in a number of circumstances that are not commonly associated with grief. Lying awake at night, ruminating over the frightful near miss on their drive home, an individual could use these letters to write to and from the offensive driver. They are unlikely to ever come across the person in reality, so the letters help them put their feelings to rest. They take care of themselves by reclaiming authority over their own comfort.

These letters are particularly useful in helping someone to quit smoking. Another client taught me this application. This middle-aged man said that he wanted to quit smoking but while he talked of the moments when he would sit with his son, sharing a drink and a cigarette, he sounded wistful. There was a melancholy to his story. Everyone is well versed on the harms of cigarette smoking, but no one mentions what people like about smoking and what they will miss if they stop.

I had clients write to the universe, a benevolent higher power, or any imagined external authority, to complain about the unfairness of having to give up something they like even though they know it is not good for them. I had them be very specific in detailing the benefits, such as: the camaraderie of connecting with strangers when asking for a light; the instantaneous buzz with that first drag; and, the thrill of rebellion in doing what was socially unacceptable. I also had them detail what they didn't like, for example: the residual taste in the mouth; the smell of their clothing; the nagging cough; and, the monetary cost! One reply letter, validating the unfairness of this dilemma, was the only response that was needed. I remember one, 45-year smoker, quitting within two weeks of completing two sets of these letters.

These letters may also be used to help with unhealthy eating habits, or drug and alcohol use. Acknowledging the loss, of the pleasures and self-medicated soothing associated with these behaviors, will honor the individuals choosing to help themselves. The letters may be written to a higher power or to the substance itself.

One young woman had problems with illicit drug use. She had recently used morphine pills to quash the emotional turmoil she was experiencing. This was long before the intensity of the opiate crisis we experience today, but was still a big concern as I was about to go away for a two-week break. I had her complete letters to the drug during the session. After writing the first letter, she began the desired response with "Hey baby." I stopped her, insisting that those words applied to the expected response of a substance wanting to ensnare her in its grip. Instead, I dictated the brutally honest reply, with the morphine telling her that it would certainly make her feel good while gradually destroying her. To her credit, she didn't use in my absence and we were able to make more progress with the therapy.

Another variation on the use of these letters is in couples work. I had each member of a couple complete the three letters and then exchange them. It was informative to each person when they were given the feedback about what they offered versus what was wanted in the relationship. This material was then processed in their therapy sessions.

I know that there are many suggestions used by therapists with regard to letter writing but I have not come across this combination of letters elsewhere. It is one thing to be able to put your feelings out there and it is a very different experience to get a reply. This is especially true when the reply is one you would like, and often need, to free yourself from that place of wanting and not receiving. I hope that you will find these letters useful in your practice.

Reference

Kopp, S. B. (1972). *If you meet the Buddha on the road, kill him: The pilgrimage of psychotherapy patients*. Palo Alto CA: Bantam Books.

Simplified practice version of the RDS Process

General instructions:

- Use this sequence of questions as you speak to the client.
- Use the appropriate pronoun when referring to the past self; a feminine pronoun is used in the outline below. The past-self pronoun is underlined to differentiate the past self from the present self.
- Have the client ask the questions of the past self (silently in their own thoughts), then have them orally relay the responses to you.
- Incorporate pauses for client consideration and response.
- Challenge limiting or false beliefs.
- Have the client come to the new conclusions themselves. By answering the questions themselves they own the responses and you avoid "yes but" dismissiveness of your statements.
- Identify the positive intent of unconsciously generated responses.

Step One: Responses as Resources

Questions a. through e. are asked directly of the client as they move into a trance state and relay their immediate experience:

a.   What is your concern? Please describe for me what you experience emotionally and physically in your body when you think of the issue.

b.   Imagine you could take those emotions and physical responses and put them outside of yourself. What image comes to mind; what do you see?

c.   Imagine immersing yourself in the image. What is it like for you - comfortable, uncomfortable?

d.   Ask the image what it is doing to you or for you, its purpose? What comes to mind?

e.   Ask the image where, when, or how it originated; when did this response become part of your experience?

f.   Talk to yourself in the past experience that comes up for you. Ask her what she would like to know, from the you now, in order to feel more okay? Ask her what she was afraid of?

Step Two: Experiential Learning

a.   What was it like to be her in that earlier moment? What did she imagine her future would be?

b.   Imagine bringing her forward in time, sitting her next to you, and showing her who she's become, her future.

c.   How did she become you? What motivated her to keep going? Who loved her?

d.   Does she feel responsible for the events that happened to her? How did she make others do what they did? Show her who those others have been over time. Does she think anyone got treated better than she did?

e.   Does she see that what she believed about herself back then may have been wrong? Show her the consequences of those erroneous, old beliefs. Have those beliefs hurt you overtime?

f.   Is she willing to apologize for those consequences? I know you may not need an apology, that you can understand that she didn't have a lot of choices, but would she like to apologize?

g.   Do you accept the apology? If you are mad at <u>her</u>, tell <u>her</u> so. Did <u>she</u> make those choices in order to cause <u>herself</u> harm overtime?

h.   How does <u>she</u> feel with that acceptance?

i.   Is there anything more <u>she</u> would like to tell you about the past experience? Feeling sad or angry about the unfairness of what happened is understandable. Take a moment to hear <u>her</u> out and let me know when you are done.

Step Three: Fusion of Experiences

a.   Again, imagining <u>her</u> sitting beside you, how do you feel side-by-side? Is there any tension or discomfort between the two of you?

b.   What does <u>she</u> know about <u>herself</u> now that <u>she</u> didn't know before? Has <u>she</u> been resilient? Show <u>her</u> the evidence of that resilience. Is <u>she</u> innocent? Did <u>she</u> have vile intent in what <u>she</u> did? Where is the evidence that <u>she</u> was not innocent? Is <u>she</u> lovable and valuable? Could <u>she</u> have become the person you are today if <u>she</u> hadn't loved <u>herself</u>? Would <u>she</u> have made as much effort as <u>she</u> did for something <u>she</u> didn't care about?

c.   Imagine sliding together like a double image focusing into one. As you come together sharing who you are with each other, <u>she</u> gets to know, in the experience of who you are today, <u>her</u> own success. No matter how vulnerable <u>she</u> was, <u>she</u> was able to figure out what <u>she</u> needed to do to keep moving forward in time to become the person you are today. And if you could figure out what you needed to do from that younger age, you are going to figure out what you need to do from now on with all the resources you have to work with now.

Step Four: Checking

Assess the client's current experience as they progressively come out of the trance state:

a.   How do you feel? Have you come together or is there a sense of separateness still?

b.   I want you to think of that past experience we were just working with? Does it feel the same? Does it feel different? If so, can you describe what has changed?

c.   I want you to think of the image you told me about when we started. Ask that image how it was trying to be useful to you? Did it succeed in it's intent to help you?

d.   Do you need that response in your life now? Do you have other ways to take care of yourself that work better for you?

e.   Give that image a hug and sincerely thank that meta-phorical response for its help when it was thought to be needed. Reassure it that you have shown yourself to be more capable of taking care of yourself than it thought you would be.

f.   Now think about the concern we started with. How do you feel now, emotionally and physically in your body, as you think about that issue?

g.   I would like you to be curious between now and our next appointment as to how you find yourself feeling and responding to events. We will go over that in our next session. That will be your evidence of change for you.

Grief Work Letter Writing Exercise

Grieving is a process of acceptance and by completing these three letters, you will be able to independently grieve, to come to an acceptance of what is and to let go of what is not. You will be able to say goodbye to what you do not want to say goodbye to. These letters are for your benefit and are not given to anyone, therefore be as open and honest as possible when writing them.

Letter One

The first letter is written to a person (dead or alive), a past self, or a benevolent higher power, and candidly expresses feelings, wants, likes, dislikes, and disillusionment felt in relation to the experience being written about. This letter must be written with all the intensity that you feel about the subject, in order for it to be useful to you.

Letter Two

Imagining the one written to has received the letter, write a second letter, a fantasy reply letter expressing your most desired response. Include in this letter words that validate your feelings and express accountability. Do not include any justifications, excuses, patronization, or use of the word "but". It may also include an apology of three parts: I'm sorry; it will never happen again; and, what can I do to make it up to you? This fantasy reply letter may be written as a simple "nice" apology or may be written as a courageously honest response, such as: "You are right. I never did like you!" Again, it must validate the feelings of the person, you, doing the three letters.

Letter Three

Again, imagining receipt of the first letter, this third letter is another reply letter, differing from the one above in that it expresses the expected response. This letter validates the knowledge and experience you have of whom you are writing to. A second reply letter is not necessary when writing to a benevolent higher power, someone deceased, or a past self, because the desired response is also the expected response.

The two reply letters separate the fantasy, the illusion of the most desired response from the reality, based on experience, of the expected response. By doing these letters, you will be able to come closer to acceptance of what is, as separate from the fantasy of what is desired, saying good-bye to illusions that result in disappointment. Acceptance is a beginning point, a solid ground from which to then move forward.

Reference

Adapted from: Kopp, S. B. (1972). *If you meet the Buddha on the road, kill him: The pilgrimage of psychotherapy patients*. Palo Alto CA: Bantam Books.

Acknowledgement

I very much appreciate the willingness of the clients who allowed me to videotape their sessions and use pieces of their therapy transcripts to exemplify the work that I have done. My son Jaime put in a lot of time and effort into reading and re-reading the initial draft of the manuscript. He provided important feedback in correcting my grammatical, structural, and stylistic errors. Drs. Jim Eliuk and Paul Schenk offered critical reviews of the book in advance of publication and I gratefully include their contributions. Sharon Meredith, R. Psych. and EMDRIA approved consultant and trainer, has told me that her "practice has benefitted greatly" from the integration of my trauma resolution protocol. As the conference chair with the Alberta Clinical Hypnosis Society, she has promoted and assisted me in workshop presentations. I imposed on my good friend, Marne Turnbull, to proof read the final draft, a chore that she eagerly agreed to do! And finally, the staff of PageMaster publishing, especially Kat my primary contact, have been very helpful and patient with my many questions, requests, changes, and corrections involved with the publication of this book. Thank you all.

https://pagemasterpublishing.ca/by/marie-wilson/

To order more copies of this book, find books by other
Canadian authors, or make inquiries about publishing
your own book, contact PageMaster at:

PageMaster Publication Services Inc.
11340-120 Street, Edmonton, AB T5G 0W5
books@pagemaster.ca
780-425-9303

catalogue and e-commerce store
PageMasterPublishing.ca/Shop

About the Author

D r. Wilson, as the developer of the trauma therapy protocol the Re-Definition of Self Process, has given workshops and paper presentations on this topic at conferences nationally and internationally since 1994. She volunteered as a board member of the Canadian Federation of Clinical Hypnosis, including two years as President, while also being a board member of the affiliated Alberta Division. She graduated from the University of Alberta in 1977, including a year of training at McMaster University in Hamilton, Ontario, prior to her Family Medicine training there. Eventually she continued postgraduate training in Marital and Family Therapy at the University of Guelph, returning to the University of Alberta to continue courses and practicums before limiting her professional practice to psychotherapy from 1987 until her retirement in 2019.

She has endeavored to live as an ancestor of the future, claiming her biggest accomplishment to be the raising of her children, Sonja, Sean, and Jaime. She takes great pleasure in seeing who they have become as citizens of the world and especial pleasure in recognizing the continuation of her influence as she watches Sean, her oldest son, being the nurturing father that he is. She continues to live in her birth city of Edmonton, Alberta.

www.ingramcontent.com/pod-product-compliance
Lightning Source LLC
Chambersburg PA
CBHW072204270326
41930CB00011B/2534